Subject-Predicate Collocations in East Asia: Focusing on Standard Korean

Subject-Predicate Collocations in East Asia:
Focusing on Standard Korean

First edition published by Seoul National University Press in 2021

Seoul National University Press
1 Gwanak-ro, Gwanak-gu, Seoul 08826, Republic of Korea
Tel: +82-2-880-5252
Fax: +82-2-889-0785
Homepage: http://www.snupress.com
Facebook: @snupress1947
Instagram: @snupress
E-mail: snubook@snu.ac.kr

ISBN 978-89-521-2990-1 (93710)

SUBJECT-

Focusing on Standard Korean

PREDICATE

Marc Duval

COLLOCATIONS

in East Asia

SNUPRESS

Table of contents

Preface and Acknowledgments

In 2006, I began to study a specific type of Korean compounds that seem to have no equivalents in European languages, that is "Subject Predicate" compounds, where "predicate" stands for either verbs or adjectives. After presenting a paper on this topic at a symposium in Paris ("$20^{\text{èmes}}$ Journées de linguistique de l'Asie orientale") in June 2006, I decided to undertake a long-term study, and started soon a 6 months long field research in Korea, at Seoul National University. This study was made possible thanks to the Korea Foundation, which endowed me with a generous grant (Fellowship for field research in Korea), from January 8th to July 8th, 2008, and to the Kyujanggak Institute of Seoul National University, where I was accepted as visiting scholar, which consequently provided me with numerous facilities. The professors of the department of Korean language and literature at Seoul National University kindly helped me in many practical and academic aspects during my stay in Korea. My special thanks go to the professors Kim Changsop and Jun Youngchul, as well as Song Jaemog (at that time working in Japan) who put me in contact with the former, as well as to Pr. Hong Chaisong. They made this stay fruitful on the scientific, professional and emotional levels.

I am also deeply indebted to three wonderful persons who always supported me from the very beginning of my studies in Strasbourg: Injoo Choi-Jonin (Université Toulouse-Le Mirail), Martin-Dietrich Gleßgen (Universität Zürich), and Alain Lemaréchal (Université Paris-Sorbonne).

Lastly, I would like to thank the following people, who accepted to share their knowledge of their native or target language during my preliminary survey, and among which are very good friends:

R. Stehly (*Arabic*); S. Bhattacharja (*Bengali*); M. Jenny, A. Vittrant, J. Watkins (*Burmese*); anon. (*Cantonese*); anon. (*Cham*); F. Siegl (*Forest Enets* & other Uralic languages); A. Malchukov (*Even*); Kalina (*Evenki*); C. Moyse-Faurie (*Futunan*); 'O. Parker-Jones (*Hawaiian*); U. Tadmor (*Hebrew*); M. Husain (*Hindi*); anon. (*Hmong*); U. Tadmor (*Indonesian*); A. Bobaljik (*Itelmen*); S. Ishida, T. Nakamura, M. Takada, R. Takeuchi (*Japanese*); E. Nyotkhampheuy (*Jruh*, Mon-Khmer); M.A.F. Klamer (*Kambera*); E. Vajda (*Ket*); T. Borgoyakova (*Khakas*); K. Sreang & J. Deth Thach (*Khmer*); J.M. Lee (*Korean*); Ph. Grangé (*Lamaholot*); N. Enfield (*Lao*); anon. (*Malay*); "Rowling" & C.G. Zhang (*Mandarin*); K. Slater (*Mangghuer*); P. Keegan (*Maori*); M. Jenny (*Mon*); Turtotogh J. (*Mongolian*); A. François (*Mwotlap*); T. Pinson (*Naxi*); I. Brill (*Nêlêmwa*); H. Shiraishi (*Nivkh*); anon. (*Persian*); T. Elidok & K. Rehg (*Pohnpeian*); M. D. Gautschi (*Romanian*); anon. (*Russian*); T. Mortensen (*Sorbung*); "Chris", "Odette" (*Tagalog*); S. Ido (*Tajik*); J. Vernaudon (*Tahitian*); M. Jenny, N. Nuangjamnong (*Thai*); F. Haller (*Tibetan*); M. Osumi (*Tinrin*); Ö. Kutbay (*Turkish*); D. Harrison (*Tuvan*); I. Nikolaeva (*Udihe*); C. Straughn (*Uzbek*); A. Dwyer (*Uyghur*); D. T. Do-Hurinville (*Vietnamese*); A. Daladier (*War*, Mon-Khmer); V. Rau (*Yami*).

Notes on transliteration

Examples taken from languages with non-Latin scripts are romanized according to the following systems:

- Chinese: pīnyīn (official romanization system of the People's Republic of China).
- Japanese: modified Hepburn system.
- Korean: Yale system.
- Thai: adapted from Mary Haas' *Essential grammar*.

-Transcription and ordinary phonetic values of vowels in Korean

<a>	아	[a]	**<i>**	이	[i]	**<uy>**	의	[ɨ(j)], [i]
<ay>	애	[ɛ]	**<o>**	오	[o]	**<wu>**	우	[u]
<e>	어	[ə]	**<oy>**	외	[we], [ø]	**<wi>**	위	[wi], [y]
<ey>	에	[e]	**<u>**	으	[ɨ]			

-Transcription and ordinary phonetic values of vowels in Mongolian

<a>	а	[a]	<o>	о	[ɔ]	<e>	э	[e]
<ye>	е	[jɛ, e]	<ö>	ө	[o]	<yu>	ю	[jU]
<yo>	ё	[jɔ]	<u>	у	[U]	<ya>	я	[ja]
<i>	и	[i]	<ü>	ү	[u]			
<i>	й	[i]	<y>	ы	[i]			

-Transcription of vowels in Thai

<-OO>	-อ	**<-uu>**	-◌ู	**<-ia>**	เ-◌ียะ
<-a>	-ะ	**<-ee>**	เ-	**<-ʉa>**	
<-a->	-◌ั	**<-e>**	เ-◌็	**<-ɛɛ>**	แ-
<-ua->	-◌ัว	**<-əəy>**	เ-ย	**<-ɛ>**	เ-◌ือ
<-aa>	-า	**<-əə>**	เ-อ	**<-ɛ>**	แ-ะ
<-am>	◌ำ	**<-ə>**	เ-อะ	**<-oo>**	โ-
<-i>	-◌ิ	**<-e>**	เ-ะ	**<-o>**	โ-ะ
<-ii>	-◌ี	**<-aw>**	เ-า	**<-ay>**	ใ-
<-u>	-◌ึ	<-O>	เ-าะ	**<-ay>**	ไ-
<-uu>	-◌ื	**<-əə>**	เ-◌ิ		
<-u>	-◌ุ	**<-ia>**	เ-◌ีย		

-Transliteration and ordinary phonetic value of consonants in Thai, Korean, and Mongolian

	Thai		Korean		Mongolian	
	Original	IPA	Original	IPA	Original	IPA
—	อ	[ʔ]	—	—	—	—
<b>	บ*	[b]	—	—	б	[p]
<c>	จ*	[tʃ]	ㅈ	[c]	ц	[ts]
<cc>	—	—	ㅉ	[c’]	—	—
<ch>	ฉ*, ช*, ฌ*	[tʃʰ]	ㅊ	[cʰ]	—	—
<č>	—	—	—	—	ч	[tʃ]
<d>	ฎ*, ด*, (ฑ?)	[d]	—	—	д	[t]
<f>	ฝ*, ฟ*	[f]	—	—	(ф)	([f])
<g>	—	—	—	—	г	[k], [G]
<h>	ห*, ฮ*	[h]	ㅎ	[h]	х	[x]
<k>	ก	[k]	ㄱ	[k], [g]	к	[kʰ]
<kh>	ข*, ค*, ฆ*	[kʰ]	ㅋ	[kʰ]	—	—
<kk>	—	—	ㄲ	[k’]	—	—

<l>	ล*, ฬ*	[l]	ㄹ	[r], [l]	л	[lʒ]
<m>	ม	[m]	ㅁ	[m]	м	[m]
<n>	ณ, น	[n]	ㄴ	[n]	н	[n]
<ŋ/ng>	ง	[ŋ]	ㅇ	[ŋ]	н	[ŋ]
<p>	ป	[p]	ㅂ	[p], [b]	п	[p^h]
<ph>	ผ*, พ*, ภ*	[p^h]	ㅍ	[p^h]	—	—
<pp>	—	—	ㅃ	[p']	—	—
<r>	ร*		—	—	р	[r]
<s>	ซ*, ศ*, ษ*, ส*		ㅅ	[s$^{(h)}$], [ʃ]	с	[s]
<ss>	—	—	ㅆ	[s']	—	—
<sh>	—	—	—	—	ш	[ʃ]
<t>	ฏ, ต	[t]	ㄷ	[t], [d]	т	[th]
<th>	ฐ*, ฑ*, ฒ*, ถ*, ท*, ธ*	[th]	ㅌ	[th]	—	—
<tt>	—	—	ㄸ	[t']	—	—
<v>	—	—	—	—	в	[v], [w]
<w>	ว	[w]	ㅗ + V	[w]	—	—
<y>	ญ*, ย	[j]		[j]	(й	[j])
<z>	—	—	—	—	з	[z]
<zh>	—	—	—	—	ж	[ʒ]

Note: Thai consonants indicated by * are transcribed in final position according to the following rules: {<b>, <f>, <ph>} → <p>; {<c>, <ch>, <d>, <th>, <s>} → <t>; <kh> → <k>; {<l>, <y>} → {n}; <h> → <Ø>.

-White Hmong tones

<-b>	high level	**<Ø>**	mid level	**<-m>**	low with final glottal
<-j>	high falling	**<-g>**	low falling breathy		
<-v>	mid rising	**<-s>**	low		

Note: VV stands for [Vŋ].

-Vietnamese tones

Register	Even	Short	Long
First	*a* mid high, level	*á* high rising	*ả* mid falling/rising (South)
Second	*à* low	*ạ* low (with glottal)	*ã* mid rising (with glottal)

List of abbreviations

Abl: Ablative
Abs: Absolutive
Acc: Accusative
Adn: Adnominalizer
Con: Connective
Cop: Copula
Dest: Destination
Dir: Directional morpheme
Erg: Ergative
Excl: Exclamative marker
Fut: Future
Gen: Genitive
Hon: Honorific morpheme
Imp: Imperative
Inst: Instrumental
Link: Linking vowel
Loc: Locative
Neg: Negative morpheme
Nm: Nominalizing morpheme
Nom: Nominative
nonFut: Non future
NumCl: Numeral classifier (sortal)
Obj: Object marker
Perf: Perfective
Plur: Plural
Pol: Politeness marker
Pres: Present
Prog: Progressive
Q: Question marker
Quot: Quotation marker
Ret: Retrospective
S: Subject
Sg: Singular
SPC: Subject-Predicate Collocation
Stand: Standard (of comparison)
Temp: Temporal adjunct
Top: Topic
TS: Terminal suffix

Introduction

Se o passa-tempo não passar o tempo, vai passar o que?
Se o cata-vento não catar o vento, vai catar o que?
Se o porta-luvas não portar as luvas, vai portar o que?
Se o guarda-chuva não guardar a chuva, vai guardar o que?

If the "pass-time" (pastime) doesn't pass time, what will it pass?
If the "search-wind" (weathercock) doesn't search for the wind,
what will it search for?
If the "carry-gloves" (glovebox) doesn't carry gloves, what will it carry?
If the "guard-rain" (umbrella) doesn't guard against rain,
what will it guard against?

O beija-flor já beijou a flor e quer beijar você

The "kiss-flower" (hummingbird) has already kissed the flower and wants
to kiss you

Se o lança-chamas não lançar as chamas, vai lançar o que?
Se o pára-raio não parar o raio, vai parar o que?
Se o pôr-do-sol não puser o sol ele vai por o que?
Se o faz-de-conta não fizer de conta, vai fazer o que?

If the "throw-flames" (flamethrower) doesn't throw flames, what will it throw?
If the "keep-lightning" (lightning rod) doesn't keep from the lightning,
what will it keep from?
If the "setting-of-sun" (sunset) doesn't set the sun, what will it set?
If the "make-account" (make-believe) doesn't make an account up, what
will it make up?

O beija-flor já beijou a flor e quer beijar você

The "kiss-flower" (hummingbird) has already kissed the flower and wants
to kiss you

Cata, porta, guarda você...
Lança, para, põe e faz você...

Search, carry, guard yourself
Throw, keep, set and make yourself

(Evandro Navarro, *Duas palavrinhas*)

1

Scope of the study

1. Preliminaries

The initial title of this study was: *Subject predicate compounds in East-Asia: Focusing on Standard Korean*. However, in the course of this study, the more examples of Korean subject-predicate frozen sequences I elicited, the more accurate and safe it seemed to call them "collocations" rather than "compounds". The contrastive perspective adopted here also suggests that it might be wiser to avoid the latter term for some languages. For instance, in prototypical isolating languages such as Thai, it seems that there is no decisive reason to distinguish between collocations and compounds (Post 2007); Nedjalkov (1997: 308) states the absence of compounds, save one single instance in the agglutinative language Evenki; Tamura (1999) considers that most Ainu compounds have the same structure as phrases (see note 21). After all, I am not sure at all that compounding is a universally known lexical (or grammatical) process. I am however fairly convinced that collocations, that is frozen sequences of words that may or may not include grammatical material, exist in all languages.

Also, the choice of "predicate", as a cover term standing for both categories of verb and adjective, in the previous title, was naturally problematic because of its wide semantic extension (e.g., nouns can rightly be considered as predicates, cf. Chap. 1, 1.1), p. 41), but I decided to keep it, instead of changing it to a simple "verb" that would have had to cover adjectives as well. In Chinese or Korean grammar, for instance, the opposition verb ~ adjective is not a primary distinction, as their overall syntactic distribution is identical.[1] However, Japanese has a morphologically and distributionally clearly distinct category of adjectives, many of which are to be found in our data. In addition, a "subject verb collocation" label should have been abbreviated to "SVC", which would have caused a rather unfortunate ambiguity with "Serial Verb Constructions". A search of the literature has failed to reveal any previous use of the terminology *Subject-Predicate collocation* in English, except as a translation of, for instance, Chinese 综述搭配 *zhǔshù dāpèi* or Korean 주술관계 연어 *cwusulkwankyey yene*. This is unsurprising given that the phenomenon itself is marginal in European languages, while it is fairly common in Asian languages. While "Subject-Predicate collocation" can be understood as a neutral and transparent descriptive phrase specifying the object of this study, the labels "European languages" and "Asian languages" should not convey such a litteral meaning: they are not meant to include *all* European and *all* Asian languages, rather those illustrated in this work, plus those bearing common typological features due to genetic inheritance and/or areal contact, as certainly is the presence or absence of Subject-Predicate collocations. It seemed therefore necessary, in order to highlight the pervasiveness of this particular feature in Asia, to give samples of languages belonging to different language families. Along with Korean –the main focus here– and English –the working language–, examples will also be drawn from other Indo-European languages on the one hand, and, most importantly, from various Asian language families on the other (Austronesian, Japonic, Mon-Khmer, Mongolic, Sino-Tibetan, Tai-Kadai).

Examples of Korean Subject-Predicate collocations (hence SPC) include sequences that often appear as single entries in usual dictionaries, such as 금가다 *kum-kata* (crack-go) 'crack, split', 겁나다 *kep-nata* (fear-arise) 'be seized with fear', 재미있다 *caymi-issta* (interest-exist) 'be interesting', and so on. This sort of combination is widely reported in Asian languages, and coexists with –from a European perspective– less unusual Object-Predicate or Oblique-Predicate compounds/collocations.

1 The compatibility with such or such inflectional morpheme does not either distinguish a specific subclass of adjectives in Korean either, contrary to what the grammatical tradition says (on this topic, Choi-Jonin & al., 1994).

Compare the following data from Korean (Ha C.K. 2002: 135, Sohn H.M. 1999), Japanese (Nomura 1977: 267, Shibatani 1990, Takada 2008), and Chinese (Li & Thompson 1981; Yip P.-C. 2000; Su Y.-Ch. 1999: §0):

	Subject	Direct Object	Obliques
Korean	'energy-enter = tiresome', *kep-nata* 'fear-arise = fear'	*yok-mekta* 'insult-eat = get insulted', *cari-capta* 'seat-take = take one's place'	*aph-seta* (front-stand) 'stand in first line'
Japanese	*me-zameru* 'eye-open = wake up', *ki-zuku* 'spirit-turn on = notice'	*na-zukeru* 'name-make = name', *yume-miru* 'dream-see = dream'	*fuyu-gomoru* 'winter-shut oneself up = hibernate', *mimi-nareru* 'ear-get_used_to = find (a sound) familiar'
Chinese	*liǎn-nèn* 'face-tender = bashful', *dǎn-hán* 'gall-cold = fearful'	*dān-xīn* 'bear-heart = worry about', *zhù-yì* 'fix-attention = pay attention to'	*qiāng-bì* 'gun-kill = execute by gunfire', *fēng-xíng* 'wind-go = be in fashion'

Concerning particularly Korean SPC, which will be the focus here, partial lists have already been established in some grammars, or in monographs devoted to word-formation in Korean (e.g. Kim J.E. 1995), but, to my knowledge, no work presenting a systematic eliciting of Korean SPC has been published up to now. It is no wonder given that the number of SPC in Korean is potentially unlimited: the process of collocating subjects is productive. A rough estimation of the number of Korean SPC that I encountered in the course of this study could reach around 500 items. Data were also gathered from other Asian languages: some are typologically similar to Korean such as Japanese or Mongolian, others are structurally very different, such as Chinese or Thai, but SPC are recorded in all of them. Note again that SPC refers here not just to all kinds of Subject-Predicate collocations or compounds, but to those that are still able to function as the main predicate of a sentence. Consider the following exemple, where the main predicate is composed of two elements: the subject argument *cam* ('sleep'), and the intransitive verb *tul.ta* ('enter'). Literally, the sentence should read as "The baby sleep entered ...".

(1) 아기가 내 옆에서 잠들었어. (Lee S.H. & al. 2016: 127)
ai.ka nay yoph.eyse ***cam.tul****.ess.e*
baby.S I:Gen side sleep.enter.Past.TS
"The baby fell asleep at my side"

Now, in order to give a glimpse of how noticeable, if not unique,[2] this kind of sentence is, one should consider a few observations concerning compounds and other kinds of frozen word-combinations. Most examples in the following sections will be drawn from European languages.

2. Compounds, noun incorporation, and idiomatic expressions

Subject-predicate collocations,[3] as well as other argument-predicate collocations may be commonly, and fruitfully,[4] viewed from three different perspectives that are all concerned with "non-free" word-combinations: noun incorporation, phraseology,[5] and compounding processes proper. A brief and rough definition of each domain is provided in the following diagram:

2 It is by no means an exception in terms of frequency.
3 "Collocation" is employed here as a generic term for compounds and idioms.
4 As a matter of fact, given that the scope and objectives of these three perspectives differ and go beyond the topic of SPC proper, they all shed a slightly different light on the topic.
5 Phraseology is meant to include works on "support verb constructions", a concept developped by M. Gross within the frame of his "lexicon grammar" (English terms corresponding to "verbes supports" include the notions of "composite predicate", "light verb", an so on, see van Pottelberge, 2007: 436). Intensive research within the frame of lexicon-grammar has been carried out on Korean (see the works of Hong C.S. & Lee S.H.).

Argument-predicate collocations (including SPC) viewed from three perspectives

Noun incorporation
or: *How the lexicon supplies syntax*

Phraseology
or: *How syntax supplies the lexicon*

Argument-Predicate Collocations

Word formation (Compounding)
or: *How the lexicon supplies the lexicon*

Noun incorporation describes a type of compounding whereby, in some specific/predictible conditions, a verb and its noun complement[6] appear as a single word, or in other words, “an N stem is compounded with a V stem to yield a larger, derived V stem” (Mithun 1984: 847). It is usually considered an integral part of the grammar of a given language, as long as this lexical process supplies what cannot be achieved through purely syntactic (i.e. analytic) combinations: the lexicon thus supplies “syntactic gaps” in grammar. Incorporating constructions differ from alternative constructions in their informational structure rather than in their referential meaning. In Chukchee, a Paleosiberian language of Northeast Asia, such Noun-Verb compounds clearly exhibit properties of single words (verbs): verb prefixes can be attached to the incorporated noun, and the whole complex is subject to vowel harmony. Noun incorporation as a kind of compounding process is specific in that there should always be an analytic, syntactically “well-formed”, variant of the synthetic noun incorporating sequence.

Phraseology is the study of frozen word-combinations, in which idiomaticity, or non-compositionality, traditionally plays a central role.[7]

6 There may be cases of ‘adjunct-incorporation’ as well, with ‘adjunct’ serving as a cover term for adverbs, adjectives, numerals, etc.

7 “Für eine Sprache spezifische Wortprägung oder [...] Wortverbindung/phraseologische

The English Verb-Noun collocation *to kick the bucket* is probably one of the most commonly quoted idioms. It is non-compositional as the meaning of the whole cannot be deduced from the meaning of its parts, as are the following equivalent expressions: Dutch *het loodje leggen* ('lay the piece of lead'), Germ. *ins Gras beißen* ('bite in(to) the grass'), Hung. *fűbe harap* (id.), Fr. *casser sa pipe* ('break one's pipe'), etc. Idioms are not, in principle, restricted as to the quality and quantity of their constituents, that is, they may involve grammatical material such as determiners, prepositions, etc., and may be as long as full sentences (e.g., proverbs: *All that glitters is not gold*). Emphasis should be given to their strongly bound and cohesive internal structure and their word-like availability for the community of speakers, together with the non-predictibility of their co-occurrence:

> "Phraseologisch ist eine Verbindung von zwei oder mehr Wörtern dann, wenn (1) die Wörter eine durch die syntaktischen und semantischen Regularitäten der Verknüpfung nicht voll erklärbare Einheit bilden, und wenn (2) die Wortverbindung in der Sprachgemeinschaft, ähnlich wie ein Lexem, gebräuchlich ist. Die beiden Kriterien stehen in einem einseitigen Bedingungsverhältnis: wenn (1) zutrifft, dann auch (2), aber nicht umgekehrt." [A combination of two or more words is phraseological, when (1) the words form a unit that cannot be fully explained on the basis of the syntactic and semantic regularities of the link, and when (2) this combination is in use, much like a lexeme, in the language community. These two criteria stand in a one-way conditional relationship: when (1) holds, so does (2), but not vice versa.] (Burger & al., 1982: 2)

To put it differently, the input of phraseology can be any kind of syntactic combination, without apparent restriction,[8] and the output has

Einheit, deren Gesamtbedeutung sich nicht aus den lexikalischen Einzelbedeutungen ableiten lässt; [...]." [For a language-specific word formation or [...] word combination/ phraseological unit, the overall meaning of which cannot be derived from the lexical individual meanings.] (Lewandowski, 1990: 268)

8 One could actually wonder whether there are not idioms above the utterance-level, for example in two-voiced interactions, but this issue is irrelevant here.

word-like properties, at least as concerns its presumable availability in the speakers' mental lexicon. In that sense, syntax supplies the lexicon.

Lastly, **compounding** is a process of word-formation through which two or more words are combined in such a way that the output sequence functions as (= has the properties of) a single word. Given this condition, compounding differs from "free combinations" of words that result in phrases or sentences. Thus compounding is generally not thought of as belonging to grammatical description proper,[9] but rather as a lexicon internal process (lexicon to lexicon). Scholars may disagree whether, and to what extent, compounds comply with the rules of syntax. At least compounds should not include grammatical words (see Scalise 1992: 196; 1994: 141). Specialists of compounds may additionally quarrel about whether non-compositionality should be listed among properties of compounds. For instance, discussing Verb-Object compounds in Chinese, Packard (2000: 118) takes it as a sufficient (but not necessary) condition while Paul (1988) considers it totally irrelevant. Whatever the claim, it might be useful to distinguish between *literal* and *idiomatic* compounds.

It is noteworthy that instances of argument-predicate sequences are found under all the above mentioned headings, but usually the verb is transitive and the argument is a direct object. Conversely, cases of Subject-Predicate collocations seem to be exceptions.

3. Subjects in idioms and compounds

An overview of the literature dealing with morpho-syntactic phenomena such as compounding, phraseology, or incorporation, most likely

9 Compounding is also seen as a non-regular, non-predictible, idiosyncratic process of word-combination. In that sense, lexical compounding differs from incorporation. Thus English verbal compounds such as *babysit* and *breastfeed* should not be seen as cases of noun incorporation. Not only are there few of them, but some are back-formations (cf. *breast-fed* and *babysitter*) rather than "synthetic alternants" of the analytical phrases *to sit a baby / to feed with breast*. See also *to wordprocess, to berrypick, to sideswipe*, etc. Still, the borders between (lexical) compounding and noun incorporation may be fuzzy. See however Launay (1998).

supports the view that objects are internal arguments most closely related to the (main) verb (see Jacob 2003). As such, they easily bind with verbs and create new lexical or phraseological units, illustrations of the former being numerous in European languages, e.g. Eng. *kick the bucket*, Germ. *jm. das Gas abdrehen*, Fr. *mordre la poussière*, etc. Whereas Cheon M.-A. (2007) includes items such as *kep.i nata* (fear.Subj arise) "to fear" (p. 767) in her presentation of Korean phraseology, most examples of idioms with subject-verb collocations that one can easily collect from the literature on European languages are full sentences with little or no ability to be expanded. See, for instance, proverbs (e.g. *You can lead a horse to water but you can't make it drink*) or sentences that describe specific events such as S.A.E. *An angel passes* (Bárdosi 1989), Germ. *Die Tante Rosa ist angekommen*, Fr. *La petite souris est passée*, etc. Like proverbs, these examples do not prove that subjects can collocate with verbs, but rather show that full sentences can be lexicalized. Observations about the inability of subjects to appear in idiomatic expressions that are not fully lexicalized include Keenan (1976) and Marantz (1984):

> "[...] there are countless object idioms in English like *kick the bucket* while subject idioms that are not full phrasal idioms are rare, if they exist at all." (Marantz, 1984: 27)

In his study of German idioms, however, Webelhuth (1995), quoting Marantz, provides evidence for the existence of subject idioms containing an open argument position. According to the author, there are only few of these (16 on 386 verbal idioms), although they outnumber idioms with a frozen indirect object (only 3, p. 409). He also points out that the frozen subjects involved are non-agentive, a fact that "invites an analysis in terms of unaccusativity which would locate the surface subject within the VP at D-structure where it can be directly theta-marked by the verb" (p. 406). Examples:[10]

10 See also Fr. *Quelle mouche a piqué X?* "Which fly has bitten X = What's bitten X" vs. *X a pris la mouche* "X took the fly = X got upset", etc.

German Subject idioms (Webelhuth, 1995: 404-405)
X raucht der Kopf (X smokes the head)
"X's head is spinning"

X brummt der Schädel (X buzzes the head)
"X's head is throbbing"

X rutscht das Herz in die Hose (X slides the heart into the trousers)
"X's heart sinks into X's boots"

Bei X ist eine Schraube locker (with X is a screw loose)
"Someone has a screw loose"

X bringen keine zehn Pferde dahin (X bring no ten horses there)
"Wild horses wouldn't drag X there"

Elements of compounds also show "underlying" predicate-argument relationships, though such an interpretation is sometimes a matter of dispute among scholars. For instance, a *truck driver* is to be understood as "(someone who) drives trucks": there is an object-verb relation between the first and the second element of the compound. Such items are sometimes referred to as "synthetic compounds" (Tomić 1998: 128). Note that the derivative suffix *-er* in *truck driver* qualifies examples of this type as illustrations of two successive word-formation processes: derivation *and* compounding, the order of which is debated. Tomić (1998: 136) lists properties of synthetic compounds, of which the fifth specifies that "the modifying constituent **can never be related to the subject** of a sentence in which the corresponding verb appears". Then she goes on to show the unacceptability of potential candidates:

John drives a truck.	→ **John-driver*	(vs. *truck driver*)
The egg is fried in a pan.	→ **egg-fried*	(vs. *pan-fried*)
The coat is worn by time.	→ **coat-worn*	(vs. *time-worn*)

Numerous instances of verb-noun compounds without initial or further derivation are also found among nominals. These are examples of the *pickpocket* type, though this type is rare in Germanic languages (Paillard, 2007: 159). Tomić (1998: 128) gives the following examples: *cutpurse, cutthroat, daredevil* (i.e. 'who dares the devil'), *pickpocket* ('who picks, i.e. robs pockets'), *sawbones, scarecrow.*[11] This is not a productive word-formation pattern in English. However, similar verb-noun compounds are widely reported in the Romance family,[12] where, given their productivity, the number of such combinations is potentially unlimited. Examples:

Language	Compound	Gloss V-(N)		Meaning
Catalan	*cobrellit*	cover	bed	'bedspread'
	escura-xemeneies	sweep	chimneys	'(chimney-)sweep'
	menjacapellans	eat	priests	'anti-clerical'
	tornaveu	turn	voice	'echo'
French	*vide-poche*	empty	pocket	'glove/map compartment'
	cache-col	hide	neck	'scarf'
	coupe-ongle(s)	cut	nail(s)	'nail clippers'
	*réveille-matin**	wake	morning	'alarm clock'
Italian	*portacenere*	bear	ashes	'ashtray'
	*girasole**	turn	sun	'sunflower'
	asciugamano	wipe	hand	'hand-towel'
	rompiscatole	break	boxes	'pain (in the neck)'
Portu-guese	*mandachuva*	summon	rain	'big shot' [Brazil]
	beija-flor	kiss	flower	'hummingbird'
	cata-vento	collect	wind	'weather vane'

11 Other items: *killjoy, spoilsport, ceasefire, cut-throat, pastime,* etc. Many of these compounds have disappeared from the modern language (Tuggy, 1987).

12 For Italian: Tollemache 1945, Bisetto 1999, Dardano 1978, Sugeta 1992, Widłak 1991; Spanish: Lloyd 1968, Tuggy 2003; French: Bierbach 1983, Arnaud 2003, Roussarie & Villoing 2003, Villoing 2002, 2003; Catalan: Hualde 1992, Verdaguer 1999; Romanian: Schapira 1985. For an overview of N-V compounding in Romance languages, see Darmesteter 1894, Giurescu 1975, Klingebiel 1989, Bork 1990, Gather 2001, Lüdtke 2005. Latin seems however depauperate of such compounds; they would in any case follow a NV pattern: *sanguisuga* (blood-suck) "leech".

Romanian	*pierde-vară* *linge-blide* *cască-gură*	lose lick open	summer dish mouth	'idler' 'penny pincher' 'absent-minded person'
Spanish	*lavaojos* *portaestandarte* *besaflores* *pasatarde**	wash bear kiss come	eyes standard flowers late (adv)	'eye cup' 'standard bearer (in cavalry)' 'colibri' (Guayana) 'latecomer'

As can be seen from the chart, the underlying structure of most items seems to be an object-to-verb relationship.[13] Examples marked with a "*" display other kinds of relationships: (temporal-)comitative (*girasole* = "turns with the sun"), temporal (*réveille-matin* = "wakes in the morning"), and even a (again temporal) adverb-to-verb relationship (*pasatarde* = "comes late"). Some authors have invoked a **"subject-constraint"**, ruling out the possibility for the noun in the V-N compound to bear a subject relation to the verb (Barbaud 1994: 9; Scalise 1994: 135). Gather (2001: 77-79) however discusses a few examples that take on a subject-to-verb relationship (It. *batticuore, battiscopa, marciapiedi, corrimano*, Fr. *croque-monsieur, croque-mitaine, gobe-mouton, pense-bête*, Sp. *andaniño, saltacaballo*). If we consider French, apart from data that are no longer analysable today, potential subject-verb compounds always seem liable to a "hidden causative" analysis. In the following examples, the causative gloss sounds more accurate:[14]

13 See also Lüdtke (2005: 274): "Am häufigsten sind die Fälle, in denen die Ergänzung in der Beziehung des **direkten Objekts** zu einem transitiven Verb steht [...]." [The most frequent situation is when the complement stands in a direct object relationship to a transitive verb]; or Basílio (1989: 29-30): "Ainda, em composições verbo + substantivo, o substantivo tem **função análoga à de objeto do verbo**: *guarda-roupa, mata-mosquito, porta-bandeira*" [In verb + noun compositions, the noun has a function analogous to that of the verb's object: wardrobe, 'kill-moskito' (mosquito killer), 'carry-flag' (flag carrier)].

14 Cf. Villoing (2003: 192): "[...] le prédicat complexe qui apparaît dans *trotte-bébé, coule-sang* et *pisse-chien* **ne s'interprète pas comme «N agent de V»** (tel qu'on l'observe dans les phrases *le bébé trotte, le sang coule, le chien pisse*), mais correspond respectivement à 'faire trotter bébé', 'faire couler sang' ou 'faire pisser chien'" [the complex predicate appearing in 'trot-baby' (baby walker), 'flow-blood' (surgical tool or viper species) and 'piss-dog' (a servant walking dogs) is not interpreted as "N agent of V" (as we observe

French	Verb	Noun	Meaning	Subject-to-verb gloss	Causative gloss
croque-monsieur	crunch	sir	(a toasted ham and cheese sandwich)	"Sir crunches (X)"	"(X makes) a sir crunch"
tourne-disque	turn	record	'record-player'	"Records turn (on X)"	"(X makes) records turn/ revolve"
pense-bête	think	fool[15]	'memory jogger'	"Fools (can) think (with X)"	"(X makes) fools think/recall"

Catalan (Adelman 2002), together with Occitan, is an exception within the Romance family in that it has productive noun-verb *verbal* compounds, of the right-headed type *ull-prendre* (eye-take) 'to catch someone's eye', *coll-portar* (neck-carry) 'to carry sg on one's neck', *cor-nuar-se* (heart-knot) 'to have a strong feeling of distress/anxiety/fear', *cor-bategar* (heart-beat) 'to have the heart beat', some of which are to be interpreted as subject-verb compounds, or at least as ambiguous constructions with respect to the relationship between the verb and its argument. As Adelman (2002: 10) notes about *peu-calcigar* (foot-step on) 'to step on with one's foot/to step on someone's foot':

> "[...] *peu*, the *foot*, can be interpreted as either that which steps on something, executing the action of the verb, or that which is stepped on, affected by the action."

It is likely that the N-V verbal compounding process was productive in early Romance,[16] as shown in Klingebiel (1989).[17] The reason it is still

in the sentences *the baby walks, blood runs, dog pisses*), but corresponds respectively to 'make baby trot', 'make blood flow' or 'make dog piss'].

15 Fr. *bête*, meaning "stupid" is normally used as an adjective not as a noun. Interpretating it as a (de-adjectival) noun here seems however the only appropriate gloss.

16 Reflexes of this pattern are still found in modern Romance languages: see Fr. *colporter* (< *cou-porter* 'wear on one's neck', a refection of o.Fr. *comporter* 'transport') or *maintenir* (< **manu-tenere* 'hold by hand').

17 For an updated discussion about the origins of this pattern, see Lüdtke (2005: 274-279):

productive in Catalan and Occitan could be related to their closeness to Basque, where this process is also documented (Hualde & Ortiz de Urbina, 2003: 357-358):

	Noun	Verb			Meaning
lan egin	*lan*	'work'	*egin*	'do'	'work'
odolust(u)	*odol*	'blood'	*hustu*	'empty'	'bleed'
itxuralda(tu)	*itxura*	'aspect'	*aldatu*	'change'	'transform'

Rijk (2008: 871) actually uses the term "incorporation" in his discussion of verbal compounds in Basque[18] and quotes a few examples with ergative arguments, that is nouns that would correspond to subjects of transitive verbs in nominative-accusative languages such as English (cf. Chap. 1, 2. 1), p. 50):

	Noun	Verb			Meaning
harjo	*har*	'worm'			'wormy, to be worm-eaten
ilargijo	*ilargi*	'moon'	*jo*	'hit'	'be moonstruck, lunatic'
itsasjo	*itsaso*	'sea'			'seasick, be seasick'
lokartu	*lo*	'sleep'	*hartu*	'take'	'fall asleep, die'
sukartu	*su*	'fire'			'catch on fire, get a fever'

Even if the process is quite productive in these languages, at least for objet-predicate sequences, one should consider that there is no regular alternation between compounded and non-compounded sequences. Basque data thus illustrates a semi-productive "noun stripping" process rather than a proper instance of noun incorporation.

At any rate, several authors point out that **subjects rarely incorporate**. As Sadock (2006: 585) puts it:

"Herkunft der Verb-Ergänzung-Komposition".

18 "In all cases of this type we are concerned with incorporation, that is, the incorporating into the verb of a noun or adjective in the neutral form, thus without an article, and mostly also without a case ending." (Rijk 2008: 870)

> "Roughly speaking, **the more like a subject a noun is, the harder it is to incorporate**; the more animate a noun is, the harder it is to incorporate; and the more definite it is, the harder it is to find a NI [=noun incorporation] structure. Potential examples such as *John-eat the meat* with *John* as an incorporated noun have not been attested."

It is actually doubtful whether proper nouns such as *John* could be incorporated in any function, be it as a direct object (*Mary likes Peter* → ??*Mary like-Peter-s*) or as an indirect object (*Peter is talking to John* → ??*Peter is talk-to-John-ing*).[19] Noun incorporation with subject nominals[20] is, however, sporadically documented:

Ainu (Tamura, 1999; Shibatani, 1990)[21]

(2) *mé-an*
coldness-exist
"It's cold."

(3) *kem-noye*
famine-twist
'starve to death'

---

19 Proper nouns referring to humans may also appear in synthetic compounds, as in *Paki-bashing* ("The activity of making vicious and unprovoked physical or verbal attacks on Pakistani immigrants living in Britain") or *Paki-basher*. Such examples once more illustrate the integration of a direct object (*to bash Paki(s)*), and probably a kind of dehumanization when humans are involved.

20 But then again there should theoretically be another constraint: so-called "unaccusative" subjects do incorporate, while "unergative" subjects do not (Nedjalkov 1976, but Polinsky 1990, 1993 for counter-examples). See *infra* section 2.1 for a brief mention of the unaccusative hypothesis.

21 Tamura (1999: 193-197, chapter entitled "word formation") does not mention examples of subject-predicate compound verbs as instances of noun incorporation. But as she puts it: "The majority of Ainu compound words have the same composition as phrases; accordingly, the analysis of compositional elements in compounds follows the same process as the analysis of compositional elements in phrases. Because of this, it can be difficult to judge whether something is a compound word or a phrase" (Tamura 1999: 193).

Chukchee (Spencer, 1999: ch. 5)

(4) *ym'yloñet ty-lewt-y-pygt-y-rkyn*
all.day 1Sg-head-hurt-Pres.I
"I've had a head ache all day."

(5) *ynqo ge-j'ilg-inini-lin*
then Past.II-moon-appear-3Sg
"Then the moon appeared."

Tuscarora (Mithun, 2000: 917)

(6) *Ka-hséhar-ahkwahst*
neuter-ash-be.good
"They are good ashes."

As we have seen above, the output of noun incoporation has, by definition, compound properties. But it also has other properties that make it a grammatical process rather than a lexical process. In particular, the alternation between noun incorporating sequences and "free" argument-verb sequences should be predictable and linked to an equally predictable semantic difference. These characteristics are not found in the data presented here, so that most of our Asian data, except in Austronesian languages, are more accurately considered "lexical compounds" rather than "grammatical compounds". In addition, it is often difficult to assess their status as compounds. The description of Korean data in this respect is particularly tricky, since a lot of properties traditionally attributed to compounds prove to be irrelevant here.

4. Problems related to the recognition of verbal compounds in Korean

In Korean, a problem lies in how one should count a given string as a SPC, since most SPC sequences may function as regular sentences with an overt marking of the subject constituent. Thus, the SPC *caymi-issta* 'interest-exist = be interesting' may show up with the subject particle *ka* without any change of meaning. The only difference lies in the focalizing effect of the subject particle:

(7) *caymi-issta / caymi.**ka** issta*
interest-exist / interest.**S** exist
"It's funny (indeed)!"

Conversely, in spoken Korean, the subject particle is frequently omitted with all types of regular subject constituents. It is thus necessary to find diagnostic criteria of *integration*. On the phonetic side, for instance, although a number of phonological transformations ('sandhi-phenomena'), such as nasalization, occur in Korean at the borders of constituents, none seem to be characteristic of compounds; nasalization can thus appear in assumed SPC (*mok-maluta* (throat-dry) 'be thirsty' [mo**ng**-maluta]), but also between phrases or affixes: e.g. *pap mek.ess.ni?* /rice eat.Past.Int/ 'Did you have your meal?' [pa**m** mek.e**n**.ni]. This behaviour contrasts sharply with Japanese SPC, which may undergo a sandhi phenomenon known as 'rendaku', a process typical for compounds whereby the first consonant of the second element becomes voiced: e.g. 腹(が)立つ *hara(.ga) tatsu* > *hara.**d**atsu* (belly(.S).stand) 'be angry'. Japanese, in addition, give hints of integration through the accentual pattern of the sequence ([ha^{rada}tsu]).

2

Significance of the study

1. Theoretical implications: Subject properties and behavior

The first and most obvious reason why SPC are of theoretical relevance for linguistics is that it is too often assumed that subject nominals do not normally participate in compounding or collocating processes, or that they are the least likely candidates for integration. In Korean, for instance, it seems that subjects come in second place as elements of compounds/collocations, after direct objects, but before indirect objects or circumstancials. Note that the absence of subject-predicate compounds (from a Western perspective) was one of the arguments supporting the analysis of subjects as external arguments (outside of the verb phrase), while direct objects are considered internal arguments (see Marantz 1984).[22]

But according to the so-called Unaccusative Hypothesis (Perlmutter 1978 and followers), there is a class of intransitive verbs (normally including adjectives), namely 'unaccusative verbs', whose sole argument, whether formally marked as a subject or not, displays object-properties and should therefore be treated as a (primary) object, or, in other theoretical frames, as an internal argument of the verb. As a matter of fact, most intransitive verbs involved in SPC are semantically close to

22 Marantz' argument that "idiomatic fixation is sensitive to relative structural position" would hold as well for indirect objects, that, given their rarity in idioms, should be given a higher structural position with respect to direct objects (Hoekstra 1991).

unaccusative verbs:[23] e.g. Kor. *ppacita* 'fall', *nata* 'appear, arise', *kata* 'go', etc. Presenting Korean and other Asian data may then prove to be of great consequence for the supporters of the unaccusative hypothesis, since Korean SPC seem to confirm that only nominals with object properties may undergo compounding. But of no less consequence is the fact that a few verbs appearing in SPC are either non-unaccusative verbs (i.e. with a regular, not object-like, subject) or even originally *transitive verbs* (i.e. with a subject and an object argument), e.g.: 귀가 먹다 *kwi.ka mekta* (ear.S eat) > *kwi-mekta* '(become) deaf'.

2. Descriptive implications: Subject-Predicate Collocations in East Asia

In a reference book on Chinese morphology (Packard 2000), compounds occupy an important place, but the relevant sections focus almost exclusively on Verb-Object compounds. In general, references about Subject-Predicate compounds in Chinese are rather scarce, perhaps because it is easier to recognize and analyze the former than the latter. SPC may nevertheless be documented in various Asian languages (see for instance Donohue 2004, Iwasaki 2002, Matisoff 1986, Yip P.C. 2000, etc.), but only for a sub-class of items, typically those which are expressions of emotions or personalities, and without a large-scale collection of data. These seminal works thus suggest the question whether Subject-Predicate Collocations in general, or rather a subclass of them, constitute an areal feature in Asia. Consequently, it is worth investigating languages, such as Korean, Japanese, or Mongolian, that are not supposed to belong to the Southeast Asian 'Sprachbund' (see Enfield 2003, Goddard 2005, Hashimoto 1976).

23 About unaccusativity in Korean, see: Kang S.Y. 1997; Kim Y.J. 1990; Lee J.K. 1998; Lee J.K. & Lee C.M. 2003; Yeon J.H. 1989, 1993, 1996. For Japanese: Fukushima 1991; Kishimoto 1996; Miyagawa 1989; Toratani 1997. A comparison of both languages in Kim J.H. 2003.

3. Lexicographic applications

Whether or not a compound or a collocation should be included in a dictionary is an urging issue for experts engaged in the making of monolingual or bilingual dictionaries. In the case of SPC, the lack of clear-cut criteria of frozenness can be supplied by a frequency study, by the lexicographer's intuition, or by other clues of integration that may only apply to a few sequences. It is hoped that the discussion brought on Korean facts in chapters 2 and 3 will help the lexicographer in this task.

3

Organization of this work

Chapter 1 is intended as a critical introduction to the main topic of this work: the first half will discuss the functional notions 'predicate' and 'subject'; the second will consider properties and diagnostic criteria related to compounds. With examples mainly drawn from Asian languages, the validity and applicability of potential properties of compounds, as listed in the following chart, will be questioned cross-linguistically:

Integration

Tier	Level	Effects
Phonology	→ Phonological proper	E.g.: *sandhi*
	→ Suprasegmental	E.g.: *accentual/tonal integration, vocal harmony*
Morphology	→ Morphological proper	E.g.: *boundedness*
	→ Semantic	E.g.: *non compositionality*
Syntax	→ Syntactic proper	E.g.: *non separability*
	→ Paradigmatic	E.g.: *non contrastivity*
Functions	→ Functional proper	E.g.: *loss of function properties (incl. marking)*
	→ Argumental	E.g.: *unpredictable change of argument frame*

Chapter 2 will then focus on the properties of Korean subjects on the one hand, and properties of compounds on the other. It will strive to show that traditional diagnostic tests for compounding either do not apply, or apply only locally or arbitrarily to Korean SPC.

In Chapter 3, emphasis will be placed on (contrastive) focalization tests, which, contrary to what is taken for granted in the literature,[24] are far from being specific to compounds. In fact, the set of elements that cannot be placed in contrastive focus is rather large. It includes at least the following: (i) minimal meaningful constituents of words (morphemes), (ii) constituents of frozen word-combinations (including compounds), (iii) discourse constituents ('disjuncts'), and even (iv) the internal constituents of most phrases, save the immediate constituents of verb phrase, i.e. most direct and indirect objects. On the other hand, constituents of non-frozen argument-predicate sequences, as well as a great number of adjuncts, may be explicitly focalized (i.e. contrasted with other elements of their paradigm: cf. *It is Tara that Mike likes, not X or Y*). It should be then borne in mind that such a test does not isolate compounds. On the contrary, it rather isolates regular, free, argument-predicate sequences. That is precisely what makes this test highly relevant for this study, since, even though there may be other, language-specific, constraints, a negative answer can tell us that a potential SPC *is not* a regular argument-predicate sequence. In other words, focalization tests do not directly prove that a given sequence is a compound or a collocation. However, once ruled out other unlikely possibilities, it will be easy to state that the candidate sequence is a frozen argument-predicate combination, hence a collocation. Claims presented here will be mainly based on Korean and Mongolian data, but hints will be given as to the cross-linguistic applicability of such tests.

It is hoped that such observations will prove helpful in understanding the morphosyntactic characteristics of subjects in the grammar of East Asian languages, but also their role in referential strategies.

---

24 E.g. Kageyama 1993, 1999.

Chap. 1

On Subjects, Predicates and Compounds in Asian Languages

1

Delimiting the frame: S, P, and C?

Identifying Subject-Predicate Compounds and/or Collocations in various languages poses specific language internal problems that are implied by the label itself. It is indeed necessary to clarify what is meant when we speak of (1) subjects, (2) predicates, and (3) compounds or collocations. As will be shown, each of these notions may be used to refer to very different structural situations, and in some cases can even be claimed to be irrelevant a notion with regard to the linguistic structure of the language described. It comes therefore as a necessity to identify and/or delimit the scope of this study, through an examination of the notions involved here.

1. Predicates: Verbs, adjectives... and nouns?

1) Verbs as typical predicates

Since the pioneering works of the Prague school, it has become legitimate to distinguish, in the organization of utterances, between what is talked about and what is said about it. The second communicative function, which aims at providing the addressee with a piece of information about something or someone, is tightly bound with the notion of "predicate". A predicate, as a logical notion, is a function that relates an entity of a set to a truth values. In a linguistic sense, it is a property that has scope over something else and for the interpretation of which one has to know what is under scope. For instance, in *Mike is walking*, "Mike" is an entity talked about whereas "is walking" is a piece of information about Mike that puts Mike in relation with the activity of walking. *Is walking* is an expression that can be true or not. If "Mike" can be interpreted without further specification, and specifically without evoking any activity, the interpretation of "is walking" necessarily involves "someone" who is walking. The word (verb) *walk* can readily be described as a logical function of the type *f(x)*, where *f* stands for the predicate (*walk*) and *x* stands for any variable that could fill in the argument place. *Walk* is thus a one-place predicate, but other verbs may have two or three slots, e.g.:

Mike is talking to Thomas. → *talk* (x = Mike, y = Thomas)
Mike put his shirt into the drawer. → *put* (x = Mike, y = his shirt, z = drawer)

In traditional linguistic descriptions, the term "predicate" is often exclusively used to refer to word categories that typically select more than one argument, and that may bear temporal coordinates, as the temporal setting is crucial to the assignment of truth values. Verbs are thus most naturally designated as predicates, since they easily select several arguments, as with the verb *put* which requires three. Note that in the example, the gerund form *walking* of the verb *walk* cannot stand alone, but is obligatorily accompanied by the auxiliary verb *be*, thus forming a compound tense called "present progressive". Since this and other compound tenses are in paradigmatic relationship with simple forms such as *walks* or *walked*, the fact that an auxiliary verb is needed for *walk* to shoulder the predicative function is usually neglected. This necessity may be considered as a grammatical trick that does not bring into question the predicative status of *walk* from a logical/semantic perspective. In compound as well as in simple forms, as a matter of fact, it still depends on the participial forms, not on the auxiliary verb, whether other elements in the sentence are required, allowed, or precluded. *Put*, for example, whether it is used with an auxiliary verb or not, requires two complements besides a subject, so that *be* (or *have*) has no role in selecting other elements in the sentence: see **Mike is putting /*

**Mike has put* / **Mike put*. The same holds for adjectives, even if, in many languages differently from verbs, they must be accompanied by a copula in order to carry the predicative function. But then again, the copula is not responsible for the number of possible or compulsory complements, see:

> *Toronto is pretty.* → *pretty* (x = Toronto)
> *Toronto is far from Mexico.* → *far* (x = Toronto, y = Mexico)

Adjectives, or what we shall refer to as "adjectival verbs", in most Asian languages just behave like verbs in not needing any implement to serve as the main predicate of a sentence.

But nouns as well, whether they need a copula or not, readily function as predicates, sometimes allowing more than one slot in their argument structure, e.g.:

> *Mike is the director of a leading company.* → *director* (x = Mike, y = leading company)

Despite the natural availability of nouns for the predicative function and the fact that in many languages nouns do not need a copula to be predicates, many linguists do not consider nouns as a word class whose function is basically predicative (see however Lemaréchal 2001). This is because nouns also typically appear in the designation of entities under the scope of *other* predicates, such as verbs and adjectives.

In this study, nouns in a predicative function will not be considered. Several reasons may lead to such a resolution, among which the most important one surely is a sudden increase in potential candidates for the SPC status. Indeed, one should then look for all noun-noun compounds in which a subject-predicate relationship could be uncovered, with the additional difficulty that both nouns may be considered the predicate of the other. Take for instance the Eng.

sequence *president-director*. Compounds of this type are not usually seen in terms of subject-predicate relationship, but they are liable to two such analyses: a president *who is a director* or a director *who is a president*. Besides, one could also take into account noun-noun compounds that can be rendered as a sentence with one noun being the subject of a prepositional phrase including the other noun. E.g., a *housewife* can be paraphrased as "a wife that [stays/is] at home [house]". As for full formed copular clauses (*X is Y*), be they of the equative (*Her name is Yoshimi*) or predicational (*She's a black belt in karate*) type, it is not expected that their subject will form a frozen combination with the predicative noun.

One consequence of this exclusion is that additional criteria will be needed in order to disqualify nouns that can appear in predicative function. Take for instance the word *blind* in its intransitive use of "being unable to see": there is no obvious functional reason why it should be encoded as a stative verb, an adjective describing a permanent quality, or a noun standing for a class of entities. In English, the fact that *blind* needs the copula *be* and no article in order to carry the main predicative function in a simple sentence (*X is blind*) implies that it belongs to the class of adjectives; conversely, it can neither get tense inflection as verbs do (**X blinded*[1]), nor take an article or a plural marker as nouns do (**X is a blind*, **X and Y are blinds*).

2) Nouns vs. verbs/adjectives in predicative function

The major problem is thus how to deal with languages in which nouns do not need a copula to function as predicates, but also how to deal in which depending on the context, may or may not show up with nouns. The following chart presents various strategies used by a sample of typologically diverse Asian languages with respect to the need of a copular element with nouns, "adjectivoids" (i.e. adjectives as a category distinct from verbs, or adjectival/descriptive verbs), and verbs.

1 Except in a transitive acception: *The dust blinded him*.

Copula use in a sample of Asian languages

	Nouns	"Adjectivoids"	Verbs	Copula
Korean	+	–	–	이다 (*i.ta*)
Japanese	+	+ –	–	Ø / だ (*da*)
Mongolian	±	±	–	байна (*bayna*)*
Chinese	+	–	–	是 (*shì*)
Vietnamese	+	–	–	?*là*
Thai	+	–	–	เป็น (*pen*), คือ (*khUU*)
Indonesian	–	–	–	Ø
Tagalog	–	–	–	Ø

Examples:

<table>
<tr><th></th><th>"T. is (a) teacher"</th><th>"T. is pretty"</th><th>+N</th><th>+A</th></tr>
<tr><td>Korean</td><td>태희는 선생이다.
Tayhuy.nun senseyng.i.ta.</td><td>태희는 예쁘다.
Tayhuy.nun yeyppu.ta.
(*i.ta)</td><td>Y</td><td>N</td></tr>
<tr><td>Japanese</td><td>タラは先生だ。
Tara.wa sensei da.</td><td>タラはかわいい。
Tara.wa kawaii (*da).
タラはきれいだ。
Tara.wa kirei da.</td><td>Y</td><td>N

Y</td></tr>
<tr><td>Mongolian</td><td>Туяа багш (байна).
Tuyaa bagš (baï.na).</td><td>Туяа хөөрхөн (байна).
Tuyaa xöörxön (baï.na).</td><td>(Y)</td><td>(Y)</td></tr>
<tr><td>Chinese</td><td>婷婷是老师.
Tíng Tíng shì lǎoshī.</td><td>婷婷漂亮.
Tíng Tíng Ø piàoliàng.
(*shì)</td><td>Y</td><td>N</td></tr>
<tr><td>Vietnamese</td><td>Tâm là giáo viên.</td><td>Tâm Ø đẹp. (*là –)</td><td>Y</td><td>N</td></tr>
<tr><td>Thai</td><td>ฐิติภรณ์|เป็น|คุณครู.
Thìtìphon pen khun khru.</td><td>ฐิติภรณ์|สวย.
Thìtìphon Ø suǎy.</td><td>Y</td><td>N</td></tr>
<tr><td>Indonesian</td><td>Tiara Ø guru.</td><td>Tiara Ø cantik.</td><td>N</td><td>N</td></tr>
<tr><td>Tagalog</td><td>Titser Ø si Tala.</td><td>Maganda Ø si Tala.</td><td>N</td><td>N</td></tr>
</table>

• Korean has the verb-like copula i.ta 'be', which is never used with verbs or descriptive verbs (i.e. adjectives).

• The same general picture holds for Japanese, with the main differences that the Japanese copula *da* does not display a regular verbal morphology (though its form varies according to tense and politeness), and that basic adjectives form a specific morphological class. That being said, *da* is not used with basic adjectives or verbs, while it is used with nouns. In addition, Japanese also possesses a class of so-called *na*-adjectives that take on nouns, in needing the copula da to access the predicative function, as in *Tara.wa kirei da* 'Tamako is pretty'. They may however differentiate from nouns when used attributively, as in *kirei.na onna* 'a pretty woman', inasmuch as the *na* allomorph of the copula in this context does not alternate with the genitive marker *no*.[2] Both types of adjectives enter subject-predicate compounds or collocations.

• In Mongolian (Kullmann & Tserenpil, 1996: 194), the existential verb *baïna* 'be, exist' can serve as a copula with both nouns and adjectives, though it is not, as a general rule, obligatory. With nouns, the copula is tense-sensitive: it is never used in the past tense and rarely in the future. In the present, *baïna* is found under two conditions only: either if the quality described by the noun is thought of as temporary, or if the state of affairs expressed has just been found out. With adjectives, irrespective of time reference, the copula is needed when the adjective expresses a temporary quality, and ruled out when it describes a permanent state.

• Chinese *shì*, which has specific properties with respect to regular verbs,[3] is necessary for nouns to function as the nucleus of a verb phrase, while adjectives, or adjectival verbs in Li & Thompson's terms (1981: 142), behave like verbs in forming verb phrases without the help of the copula. Adjectives however rarely occur alone in predicative function,

---

2 The whole picture is actually more complex, with many borderline cases. Note also that Korean and Japanese also display 'adjectivoïds' borrowed from Chinese that always need a copula. These are adjectives derived from nouns with the help of the morpheme –*teki* (Jap) or –*cek* (Kor.), corresponding to the Chinese genitive particle 的 *de*. E.g., Kor. 그는 적극적이다 *ku.nun cekkuk***cek.i***.ta* / Jap. 彼は積極的だ *kare.wa sekkyoku***teki. da** 'He's positive/active'. The same pattern may occur in Chinese with the copula *shì*, in which case the pattern is understood as elliptical, i.e. involving an unexpressed noun: 他是积极的*tā* ***shì*** *jīj***íde** 'He's an active *one*.'

3 For instance, it cannot co-occur with aspect markers, nor be negated by *méi* (*yǒu*) (Li & Thompson, 1981: 148).

and usually require either a degree adverb such as 很 *hěn* 'very', the final clitic 了 *le*; they may otherwise occur in a reduplicated form.

• The case of Vietnamese is less clear. The morpheme *là* is traditionally analyzed as a copula, since it is used in equative or attributive sentences involving predicative nouns. It does not occur with simple descriptive verbs, but it can be optionally inserted in a sequence involving a reduplicated adjective (*Tâm đẹp đẹp là* or *Tâm đẹp ơi là đẹp* 'How beautiful T. is!'[4]) or an adjective modified by a degree adverb (*Tâm rất là đẹp* 'T. is very beautiful indeed'), in contexts resembling those in which Chinese most naturally uses adjectival verbs. The copula status of *là* is actually doubtful: other uses (as well as placement rules) point to a rhematizing function of the following constituent, as before a direct object in (8) or a prepositional phrase in (9) (cf. Do-Hurinville, 2007, 2013):

(8) *Tâm thích nhất **là** sô cô la.*
T. like most Rhem chocolate
"Tam likes chocolate most of all."

(9) *Họ gặp nhau lân cuối **là** ở Zurich.*
6P meet together time end Rhem in(/live) Zurich
"They last met *in* Zurich."

The occurrence of *là* in nominal copular sentences may well reflect the fundamental asymmetry in terms of informational load between subject nouns and predicative nouns in positive copular patterns[5]: only the latter bear new information, even if N1 and N2 are referentially identical. Hence the reversibility of noun phrases in equative clauses:

4 *ơi* is an exclamative marker.

5 Negative copular sentences are not expected to follow the same pattern as their positive counterpart, as the predicative noun is not, or very much less, rhematic. In Vietnamese, negation of predicative nouns also involves *là*, in addition to the verb *phải* 'be correct' and *không* 'not': *Tâm không phải **là** giáo viên* 'T. is not a professor'.

(10) *Hà Nội **là** thủ đô của Việt Nam.*
*Thủ đô của Việt Nam **là** Hà Nội.*

Ha Noi Rhem capital of Vietnam
capital of Vietnam Rhem Ha Noi

"Ha Noi is the capital of Vietnam."
"The capital of Vietnam is Ha Noi."

The informational asymmetry however remains, and licenses the use of *là*.

• Thai displays the same contrast as Korean or Chinese, in that only nouns need a copular element. As Post (2008: 342) puts it:

> "In terms of basic distribution, verblike property concepts – like all active and stative verbs in Thai – occur as intransitive predicates [...], and do not usually occur as copula complement [...]. Conversely, nounlike property concepts – like all concrete and abstract nouns in Thai – occur as the complement of an attributive copula or other, similarly predicative functor [...], and do not usually occur as an intransitive predicate [...]."

Thai is however exotic within this sample of languages (but the same phenomenon is observed in Lao and Cambodian) in having not one but two copulas. One, เป็น *pen*, is used when the copula complement is a characteristic of the subject, as in the example above ("be a teacher"), while คือ *khUU* occurs in sentences where the subject is equated with the referent of the copula complement (e.g. "be that person"). Hence the semantic dichotomy suggested by Kuno & Wongkhomthong (1981) opposing 'characterizational' to 'identificational' sentences, and further elaboration by Takahashi & Shinzato (2003), who take into account critics made by Komolwanig & Sawada (1993).

• Lastly, Indonesian or Tagalog are known for lacking a copula, either with nouns or adjectivoids. For these languages, or those in which the copula is optional with nouns and adjectives, it is necessary to take additional criteria. Some are readily available, such as the form of the negation in Indonesian. Thus, if the predicative part of a sentence contains a noun, the negative word *bukan* is used, while verbs and adjectives are negated by *tidak* (Sneddon, 2000: 80):

(11) *Dia* ***bukan*** *teman saya.*
3P Neg friend 1P
"She isn't my friend."

(12) *Dia* ***tidak*** *sakit/bekerja.*
3P Neg sick/work
"She isn't sick/working."

The example sentences proposed above should thus be negated as *Dia bukan guru* and *Dia tidak cantik* respectively ('She's not a teacher/ she's not pretty').

Nouns in predicative function are excluded from this study, but some borderline cases may be taken in consideration if the whole sequence is worth taking into account from a contrastive point of view.

2. Subjects in Asian languages

Identification of subjects has been a matter of intense dispute among linguists for decades, and the assumption that the notion 'subject' is a universal one is seen by many as highly controversial. In most languages illustrated here, one can posit a category 'subject' without much difficulty, though in terms that may be slightly different from those assumed for languages such as English; in some other languages, this category may however be close to irrelevance.

Let us first consider subjects within the morphosyntactic system they belong to, that is, in terms of their 'morphosyntactic alignment'. Morphosyntactic alignement refers to the way languages treat ("encode") the sole argument of an intransitive verb with respect to the two core arguments of a transitive verb.

1) Alignment

Two clear and common types of morphosyntactic alignments are the (nominative)-accusative and (absolutive)-ergative types. In the former, the sole argument of any intransitive verb (S) gets the same marking as the most agentive argument (A) of a transitive verb, while in the latter, it gets the same marking as the less agentive argument (P like "Patient"). The following illustrates these two clear-cut, though somewhat idealized, situations.

(i) Accusative alignement (S/A~P)

S		**(intransitive verb)**
A	**P**	**(transitive verb)**

Latin:

(13) *STULTUS in tenebris ambulat.*
fool:Nom in shadows walk:3P
"The fool walks in the shadows."

(14) *Non recipit STULTUS verba prudentiæ:* [...].
Neg accept:3P fool:Nom words:Acc caution:Gen
"The foolish do not accept words of caution, [...]."

(ii) Ergative alignement (S/P~A)

	S	**(intransitive verb)**
A	**P**	**(transitive verb)**

Tibetan (Beyer 1992: 259):

(15) *SLOB-DPON-Ø Ngyod.*
"The TEACHER grieves."

(16) *slob-ma-s SLOB-DPON-Ø mthoń.*
"The pupil sees THE TEACHER."

Dyirbal (Dixon, 1994: 161)

(17) *ŊUMA banagan*^{y}*u.*
Father:Abs return.nonFut
"FATHER returned."

(18) *ŊUMA yabu.ŋgu bura.n.*
Father:Abs mother.Erg see.nonFut
"Mother saw FATHER."

True ergative languages are actually reported to be rare, and it is often the case that the ergative pattern is restricted to some specific grammatical context. It can be conditioned by features such as tense (Hindi) or person (Dyirbal: 3rd person arguments exhibit an absolutive-ergative alignement while 1st and 2nd persons follow a nominative-accusative patern). Such languages are said to show split-ergativity.

Unsurprisingly from a semantic point of view, synthetic idioms in ergative languages may involve the "subject" of a transitive verb: namely what corresponds in nominative-accusative systems to the most *patient*-like argument of the verb. Bresnan (2001: 13) quotes the following idioms in the Australian language Dyirbal (examples provided by "Bob Dixon with the assistance of Avery Andrews"):

(19) *buŋgu+bana-l*
knee+break = 'bend over, fold'

mala+wuga-l
hand+give = 'give a hand to, help'

miyay+yambu-l
smile+pull = 'make smile, laugh'

In these three examples, the noun stem semantically corresponds to the patient argument of the transitive verb (i.e. an object in accusative languages), even if in terms of morphological marking in non-frozen expressions, it would get the same (zero) marking as the sole argument of an intransitive verb (i.e. what would be a subject in accusative languages).

This kind of "subject" will be excluded from this study. The fact that it parallels the behavior of objects of transitive verbs in accusative languages just supports the claim made for the accusative languages that subjects are dispreferred in verbal compounds or idioms, not because they are (un)marked as subjects, but because they are Agents.[6]

(iii) Active-stative alignement (S^A/A~S^P/P)

S^A	S^P	(intransitive verb)
A	P	(transitive verb)

In still another morpho-syntactic type ("Active-stative" or "split-S"), the marking of the sole argument may either take on the transitive agent or the transitive patient, in accordance with the subcategorization of the intransitive verb. For example in Acehnese:

Acehnese (Durie 1987: 369):

(20) *GEU=jak gopnyan* — *gopnyan rhët(=GEUH)*
3Sg:Agent=go s/he — s/he fall(=3SG:Patient)
'S/HE goes' — 'S/HE falls' (ibid.)

(21) *GEU=poh=GEUH*
3Sg:Agent=hit=3Sg:Patient
'S/HE hit HIM/HER'

In such languages, two classes of intransitive verbs are to be distinguished. The distinction may be grounded on semantic features such as control, affectedness, etc., and proves to rely on a highly language-specific categorization (see Andréasson, 2001).

6 Cf. Bresnan (2001) contrasting Dyirbal and English: "in each case the noun stem corresponds to the patient argument of the verb: [...] In English this argument would be an object of the verb, but in Dyirbal, it is the subject. [...] In each case, it is the hierarchy of roles in argument structure rather than the hierarchical position of arguments in the syntactic tree that constrains idiom formation."

Within the sample of Asian languages that constituted the raw data of this study, a few display, consistently or not, ergative patterns such as Tibetan, Hindi-Urdu, or Pacific languages. Other belong to other types, such as Philippine-type languages, and most can be (negatively) classified as non-ergative languages. Such are Chinese, Korean, Japanese, Mongolian, Thai, etc. As long as they seem to display an oppositive marking of S/A arguments vs. P arguments, they can be classified as accusative languages. But as already mentioned, pure types do not exist, and some specific contexts may further complicate the overall picture. Three main situations will be presented in the following section:

(i) an occasional alignment of P with S
(ii) an occasional alignment of S with P
(iii) the stacking of S arguments

2) Inconsistencies within the general morphosyntactic alignment type

(i) Occasional alignment of P with S

In accusative languages, the distinction between S/A and P can be blurred in some specific cases, for example when one member of the pair is "zero-marked", while the other "loses" its marking. For instance, Modern Mongolian non pronominal (S/A) subjects, in main sentences, are morphologically unmarked,[7] whereas P arguments take the accusative case *-(VV)g* only if they have a specific reference (a phenomenon known as 'differential object marking', see Bossong 1985; Guntsetseg, 2009). There is, thus, no morphological distinction between an A argument and a non-specific P in transitive sentences, as in (24):

7 Standard Mongolian is sometimes said to be on the path to acquiring a subject marker: the morpheme бол *bol*, from болох *bolox* 'become'.

(22) МӨНХДӨЛ амр.ав.
Mönxdöl.Ø amr.av
Mönhdöl.Nom rest.Past
"MUNKHDUL rested."

(23) МӨНХДӨЛ мор-ийг ав.ав.
Mönhdöl.Ø mor.iïg av.av
Mönhdöl.Nom horse.Acc take.Past
"MUNKHDUL took the horse."

(24) МӨНХДӨЛ НОМ унш.ив.
Mönhdöl.Ø NOM.Ø unšiv
Mönhdöl.Nom book.Ø read.Past
"MUNKHDUL read a BOOK."

This results in a co-existence of two systems: one is the accusative system (S/A~P), the other is a non-aligned system (S/A/P), in which S, A and P are equally (zero)-marked, at least from a morphological point of view. Ambiguity does however rarely occur, due to to the lexical information given by the subcategorization frame of the verb, which is also consistently marked for voice and diathesis (Mongolian has a rich morphology in this area). In addition, when two core arguments of a transitive verb both occur in a sentence, the P argument is normally the first constituent preceding the verb. This is due to the fact that Standard Mongolian quite consistently follows an SOV pattern.

(ii) Occasional alignment of S with P

Generally speaking, even in languages that are believed to belong to the accusative type, arguments of a subclass of intransitive verbs may display object properties.

In English, non-pronominal core arguments are only marked by position, i.e., preverbal or postverbal. English is an accusative language since arguments of intransitive verbs are normally preverbal, as are the most agentive arguments of transitive verbs. Sole arguments of intransitive verbs may however occasionally appear in postverbal position: specifically, but not only, with verbs that are usually referred to as 'unaccusative verbs'. Locative inversion, for instance, can thus occur with a prototypical unaccusative verb (*appear*), as well as with a prototypical unergative verb (*swim*) (Levin & Rappaport, 1995: 218, 225):

(25) In the distance *appeared the towers and spires* of a town which greatly resembled Oxford. (L. Bromfield, *The Farm*)

(26) Inside *swam fish* from an iridescent spectrum of colors... (J. Olshan, *The Waterline*)

Chinese, too, is described as a preverbal subject language. It differs from English in having no morphological marking of any kind for a subject constituent and no agreement. However, as in English, Chinese may treat the sole arguments of certain verbs, such as those describing the occurrence of an event, as "objects". The following examples illustrate a VS order when referring to the falling of rain, the existence or disappearance of something or someone, etc. Cf. (Paul 1988: 200):[8]

(27) 下雨了
xià yǔ le
go:down rain Part
"It's raining."

(28) 刮风了
guā fēng le
blow wind Part
"The wind is blowing."

(29) 生了人
shēng le rén
bear Perf person
"Somebody was born."

8 "The following sentences seem to be problematic for the BC because here the postverbal position is occupied by a NP which apparently plays the role of the subject." (Poul 1988)

(30) 来了五个人
lài le wǔ gè rén
come Perf 5 NumCl person
"Five people came."

(31) 昨天死了三棵树
zuótiān sǐ le sān kē shù
yesterday die Perf 3 NumCl tree
"Three trees died yesterday." (Hou 1979: 21)

(32) 今天早上逃了一个犯人
jīntiān zǎoshang táo le yi ge fànrén
today morning escape Perf 1 NumCl criminal
"One prisoner escaped this morning." (Hou 1979: 30)

This occasional marking of the sole argument of an intransitive verb as the P argument of a transitive verb makes accusative languages take on active-stative languages. But it should be borne in mind that the similarity is only partial: in English as well as in Chinese, there is no consistent opposition between two classes of intransitive verbs that would each require one and only one morphological or syntactic marking to their sole argument, as should be the ideal case in active-stative languages. On the contrary, if one considers the full array of constructions of a given so-called unaccusative verb, it will prove able to enter two competing constructions, the choice of which does not only depend on its lexical subcategorization. It will also depend on the lexical subcategorization of the argument (e.g. animate ~ inanimate[9]), its definiteness (definite ~ indefinite), or its informative load (thematic ~ rhematic). That the same verbs in Chinese can also follow the expected accusative pattern is illustrated in the following sentences:

9 E.g., for Rappaport & Levin (1995), verbs of spatial configuration occur in locative inversion with *inanimate* subjects only.

(33) 他来了吗?
tā lái le mā
he come Perf Q
"Did he come?"

(34) 一 條 狗 死 在 他 家。(Zhang 2011)
*yi tiáo gǒu **sǐ** zài tā jiā*
1 NumCl die in his home.
"A dog has died in his home."

In the last example, taken from Zhang's study (2011) on the acquisition of locative inversion in Chinese, the preverbal position of the subject is said to be the canonical and unmarked order. The range of "naturally" inverted constructions seems however wider in Chinese than in English. For instance, meteorological clauses such as *xià yǔ le* 下雨了 'It rains' and *guā fēng le* 刮风了 'The wind blows', are most natural in the inverted order, thus more canonical in the VS order. For these combinations, the SV order, except for poetry, does not seem to give a well-formed sentence by itself. Two informants suggested to add a complement of duration such as in: 雨下了一夜 *yǔ xià le yī yè* 'It has rained for one night'.

(iii) Stacking of S arguments

Lastly, one should consider structures in which two arguments superficially marked as S can appear in the same sentence. Perhaps the most quoted sentence for illustrating this phenomenon is the famous sequence *Zō.wa hana.ga nagai* 'Elephant.Top – nose.S – be_long', originally presented by the Japanese linguist Mikami (1960).[10] Similar

10 Who actually argued against the use of the notion 'subject' in Japanese grammar, since important subject properties known for European languages –notably non optionality and unique assignment– are not met in Japanese. It is not debatable that Japanese as well as Korean 'subjects' differ from subjects in European languages, yet there is an homonymous marking for S/A constituents, thus a subject marking in a broad but constrained sense. This claim does not root in a belief that the notion 'subject' is necessarily a universal one, and does not imply that subjects should have the same properties everywhere. Indeed, it seems unquestionable that even in genetically and/or typologically similar languages (e.g. English and French, or Korean and Japanese),

patterns can be found in other Asian languages as well:

Japanese	象は *zō.wa*	鼻が *hana.ga*	長い *nagai* (Mikami 1960)
Korean[11]	코끼리는 *khokkili.nun*	코가 *kho.ka*	길다 *kil.ta*
Chinese	象 *xiàng*	鼻子 *bízi*	长 *cháng*
Thai	ช้าง *cháŋ*	งวง *ŋuaŋ*	ยาว *yaaw* (Iwasaki & Ing-kaphirim 2005: 360)
	'elephant'	'nose/trunk'	'long'

The Japanese and Korean sentences display a sequence of two nominals in a part-whole relationship (nose ~ elephant) followed by an intransitive predicative element qualifying the second noun. In the most regular pattern, the first nominal normally gets a Topic marking (Jap. *wa* and Kor. *nun*), while the second is marked as a subject (Jap. *ga*, Kor. *ka/i*). Such a pattern is often translated as "As for X, its Y is Z". In 'topic-prominent' languages such as Japanese or Korean, it can be claimed that the subject markers *ga* and *ka* are used for marking rhematic subjects only, while *wa* and *nun* mark topical subjects or other constituents. The first nominal can also get the subject marker, in which case there would be an implicit contrastive interpretation ('It is elephants that have a big nose').

Given that the basic alignment pattern of these languages is of the accusative type, it is not expected that two constituents in a sentence get the same "nominative" marking. As a matter of fact, the alignment type of a given language can be attributed only when there is a clear opposition between intransitive patterns with a sole argument and transitive patterns with two distinguishable arguments. Here, we seem

---

'subjects' *never* display the same properties, just as would any other functional constituent. See chapter 2 for an assessment of subject properties specific to Korean.

11 The Korean word for 'elephant' is precisely formed on *kho* 'nose' and *kil-* 'long' plus a nominalizing suffix *–i* (and tensification of the first C of the second element: $k \rightarrow kk$), so that 'elephant' in Korean is 'the long-nosed'.

to have an intransitive pattern with two undistinguishable arguments. As this construction is a typical syntactic locus for the emergence of Subject-Predicate Collocations, it will be worth discussing at length some issues related to the recognition of both the subject function and the intransitivity of verbs implied in this type of construction.

3) On double subject constructions

Interestingly enough, the subject status for the two wanna-be subjects has been a matter of dispute among linguists, obviously disturbed by the co-existence of two subjects in the same sentence.

For instance, the first nominal has been analyzed by some authors as a reduced deep-structure genitive phrase (Hashimoto 1971, Tang 1972), according to the following transformation rule:

tā bízi 'he - nose' ← *tā de bízi* 'he Gen nose = his nose'

Critics have been raised against this transformational view, bringing forth examples that do not have genitive counterparts, or that have different properties with respect to adverbial insertion (see Teng 1974: 468, and other references cited in Chappell 1996: 486-487), as respectively illustrated in (35) and (36):

(35)	他肚子饿	他的肚子饿
	Tā dùzi è.	?*Tā de dùzi è.*
	P3 stomach hungry.	P3 stomach hungry.
	'He is hungry'	'His stomach is hungry'[12]

12 This second pattern, with a genitive phrase, was judged as more acceptable than the first one by a Chinese informant living in Malaysia. Opinions of Chinese speakers living in China actually vary much: some say that both are common, others prefer the first pattern. W. Behr (pers. comm.) points to a plausible interference from other Sinitic languages such as Hakka or Min varieties. He also points out the possible acceptance of (36b) to younger speakers if the adverb *yòu* were placed in front of the verb (*Tā de tóu yòu téng le*).

(36)	他又头痛了	他的又头痛了
	Tā yòu tóu tòng le.	**Tā de yòu tóu téng le.*
	P3 again head ache PFV	P3 Gen again head ache PFV
	'He has a headache again.'	'He has a headache again.'

Similar observations have been made for Korean by Nam J.-S. (1996: 63, 117, 129sq), who contrasts the acceptability of the following sentences and points out the unnaturalness of several "genitive conversions":

(37)	✓민우가 머리가 크다.	✓민우의 머리가 크다.
	Minwu.ka meli.ka khuta	*Minwu.uy meli.ka khuta*
	M.S head.S big	M.Gen head.S big
	"M. has a big head"	"M.'s head is big"
(38)	✓민우가 머리가 어질어질하다.	?*민우의 머리가어질어질하다.
	Minwu.ka meli.ka ecilecilhata	*Minwu.uy meli.ka ecilecilhata*
	M.S head.S dizzy	M.Gen head.S dizzy
	"M. feels dizzy in her head"	"M.'s head spins"
(39)	✓민우는 등이 가렵다.	??*민우의 등이 가렵다.
	Minwu.nun tung.i kalyepta	*Minwu.uy tung.i kalyepta*
	M.Top back.S itch	M.Gen back.S itch
	"M. feels itchy in her back"	"M.'s back itches"
(40)	✓민우는 등이 반듯하다	✓민우의 등이 반듯하다
	Minwu.nun tung.i pantushata	*Minwu.uy tung.i pantushata*
	M.Top back.S straight	M.Gen back.S straight
	"M. has a straight back"	"M.'s back is straight"
(41)	✓민우는 목이 마르다.	?*민우의 목이 마르다.
	Minwu.nun mok.i maluta	*Minwu.uy mok.i maluta*
	M.Top throat.S dry	M.Gen throat.S dry
	"M. has a dry throat (= M. is thirsty)"	"M.' throat is dry (= M. is thirsty)"

As can be seen from the given examples, the "genitive conversion" is often unnatural with inalienable possessions such as body parts, especially when the sequence takes on an idiomatic meaning.

On the other hand, when the second 'subject' is an alienable possession, the genitive construction is generally grammatical, as in (42), but when the predicate states the existence or non-existence of an entity, the difference in presuppositional setting rules out any transformational equivalence (43):

(42)	내가 차가 고장난 이유는...	≈ 내 차가 고장난 이유는...
	nay.ka cha.ka kocangna.n iyu.nun	*nay cha.ka kocangna.n iyu.nun*
	I.S car.S break_down.Adn reason.Top	I:Gen car.S break_down.Adn reason.Top
	"The reason why my car broke down..."	"The reason why my car broke down..."

(43)	내가 차가 없는 이유는...	≠ 내 차가 없는 이유는...
	nay.ka cha.ka eps.nun iyu.nun	*nay cha.ka eps.nun iyu.nun*
	I.S car.S not_exist.Adn reason.Top	I:Gen car.S not_exist.Adn reason.Top
	"The reason why I don't have a car..."	"The reason why my car is not here..."

The semantic relationships involved in double subject constructions are diverse, and it is expected that different patterns will display different grammatical behaviours. Languages may also differ in the kind of patterns allowing double subject constructions. For instance, Lehonkoski (2000: 79sq.) presents a typology of potential topic-subject sentences and contrasts English, Chinese, and Korean:

Relationships between topic and subject	English	Korean	Chinese
topic = subject	×	×	×
topic and subject distinct	×	×	×

topic ~ subject			
attributed - attributing part	-	×	×
possessor - possessed	-	×	-
location - existent	-	×	×
class - member	-	×	×
scope - entity within it	-	×	×
experiencer - phenomenon	-	×	-

As she points out (Lehonkoski 2000: 79), "Unlike Korean, Chinese do not use topic-comment structures for expressing possession or existence in a location. These are formed with the verb *yǒu* 'have' that produces transitive sentences [...]." and "There is [...] one option that is open in Korean but which seems to be blocked in Chinese. Experiential sentences of the type 'I, snakes are frightening', or 'He, sleep entered' are not a Chinese pattern. Instead, transitive constructions are employed." Thus, while Chinese experiential sentences display a transitive(?) construction, Korean consistently follows a Topic-Subject pattern (the pseudo-literal translation for Korean is mine):

	Chinese	Korean
A	我喜欢他. *wǒ xǐhuan tā.* I like him "(*ib.*)"	나는 그가 좋다. *na.nun ku.ka cohta.* I.Top he.S good "As for me, he is good"
B	我怕蛇. *wǒ pà shé.* I fear snake "I'm afraid of snakes"	나는 뱀가 무섭다. *na.nun pay.ka musepta.* I.Top snake.S fearful "As for me, snakes are fearful"
C	他睡着了. *tā shuì zhuó le.* He sleep Resultative Part "He fell asleep"	그는 잠이 들었다. *ku.nun cam.i tulessta.* He.Top sleep.S entered "As for him, sleep entered"

These experiencer clauses are worth contrasting because in the Korean patterns displayed in A and B, or their Japanese counterparts, it is rather the subject status of the second constituent that has constantly been under discussion. Kuno (1973) was probably the first to consider constructions with a psychological predicate as involving "transitive adjectives" with "nominative objects". His arguments, based among others on honorific and animacy agreement as well as anaphoric binding, brought him to the conclusion that only the first constituent has subject properties. In other terms, only the first constituent is presumed to (i) select the honorific marking on the predicate, (ii) select the auxiliaries *iru* or *aru* (according to whether the subject is animate or inanimate), and (iii) control the reflexive anaphoric *jibun*. Kuno and Johnson (2005) defend this position against counter-arguments raised by Shibatani (2001). They claim for instance that the impossibility to mark honorification on the adjective (prefixation in *o-*) when the second subject, but not the first, could be the target of honorification, is a proof that it is not a subject:

(44) **Watashi.ga sensei.ga **o**-suki da*
I.S professor.S Hon-fond_of Cop
"I like the professor."

According to them, examples of such 'non-canonical double nominative constructions' stand in striking opposition with other 'double nominative' sentences, such as in the passive voice, which they consider a genuine double subject construction:

(45) *Hanako.ga otoosan.ga kootsuujiko.de **o**.nakunar.i_ni_nat.ta*
Hanako.S father.S traffic_accident.Loc Hon.die.Hon.Past
"Hanako('s) father has been killed in a traffic accident."

Similar claims have been made and challenged for Korean. For instance, the fact that the Korean honorific marker *si* only agrees with the first subject in canonical constructions is inaccurate. Park B.S. (2001) shows examples of agreement with a (possessor) genitive phrase, as with *halapeci* "grandfather", in:

(46) 할아버지의 안경이 멋지시다.
*halapeci.uy ankyeng.i mesci.***si***.ta*
grandfather.Gen glasses good_looking.Hon.TS
"Grandfather's glasses are good-looking."

The author also mentions cases of the so-called reflexive pronoun *caki* referring to the second subject as well, as in (48) (versus (47). Note that this variation in scope occurs in sentences with a psychological reference (word-by-word glosses have been adapted):

(47) *Okca*$_i$*.ka swuni*$_j$*.ka caki*$_{i/*j}$ *cip.eyse ceyil musew.ess.ta.*
Okcha.Top Swuni.S self house.Loc most fearful.Past.TS
"Okcha was most afraid of Swuni in her family."

(48) *halapeci*$_i$*.nun swuni*$_j$*.ka caki*$_{i/j}$ *pan.eyse ceyil coh.usi.ta*
grandfather.Top Swuni.S self class.Loc most good.Hon.TS
"Grandfather$_i$ likes Swuni the most among his/her classmates (lit. in his/her$_{i/j}$ class)"

It is nevertheless true that in some double nominative constructions –the non-canonical ones–, the first constituent rather than the second one *tends to* control honorific agreement and anaphoric binding, whereas the opposite situation can be observed in canonical constructions.

This point does however not imply that the second constituent of the latter pattern is an object. Firstly, it leaves open the question why there is a morphosyntactic alignment of the second constituent on the first. Secondly, it does not show that the so-called "nominative object" has object properties. Unfortunately, tests for the object function are even less consistent than those for the subject function in the languages mentioned.

Mok J.S. (2005) defends a generalized analysis of the second constituent as an object in all kinds of double nominative sentences.[13] His arguments are based, first, on the general constraint that core

13 We had a long and friendly discussion on this topic in Feb. 2009.

functions and/or thematic roles are to be assigned only once in a sentence (2005: 76); second, on the observation that there are no Subject-Predicate collocations in European languages corresponding to those found in Korean (*ibid.*, 86-87). He contrasts for instance the following collocations:

(49) 맛이 좋다 *mas.i cohta* (lit. 'taste.S good') vs. *taste good, have a good taste*;

가격이 비싸다 *kakyek.i pissata* ('price.S expensive') vs. *be high in price, be expensive, be high-priced*;

땀이 나다 *ttam.i nata* ('sweat.S appear') vs. *sweat, perspire*, etc.

It is true that Korean nominative-nominative constructions may correspond to transitive patterns in European languages, but the translated items presented here are not precisely representative of a transitive pattern. As can be seen in the chart, functional equivalents of Korean SPC may be rendered by copula complements (simple or complex adjectival phrases: *expensive, high-priced, high in price*), intransitive verbs (*sweat*) or verbal locutions in which the complement is far from being a prototypical object: it is an adverbial adjective in *taste good*, whereas the complement of *have* in *have a good taste* does not display essential properties of regular objects (cf. proportionality with the neutral pronoun *it* or passivization).

This is surely no coincidence. For the most productive nominative-nominative constructions in Japanese or Korean, namely possessive or experiencer constructions, one can readily observe that the corresponding patterns in English or French do not involve prototypical nominative-accusative arguments in terms of their morphosyntactic properties.

For example, passivization may give impossible or unnatural sentences with the complements of verbs like *have*[14] or *like/fear*:

(50) *Mike has a dog.* → **A dog is had by Mike.*

(51) *Mike likes/fears Tara.* → *?Tara is liked/feared by Mike.*

In addition, subjects of possessive or experiencer clauses are known to get unconventional markers across languages.[15]

Such phenomena point to a certain indeterminacy in the exact status of both arguments in psychological constructions. This status may not be properly captured by the notions subject and object together with their prototypical morphosyntactic properties.

The case of psychological adjectives is probably one of the trickiest instance of double subject constructions. If agreement properties tendencially qualify the first subject as a controller subject, there is one property which is undecidable, namely the primary orientation of the predicate.[16] In other terms, the question whether the predicate primarily qualifies the first or the second argument: in an example like X.*ka* Y.*ka* *cohta*, which can be translated as 'X likes Y', does *cohta* refer *first* to the state of the experiencer X (the one who likes), or to a quality of Y (the one which is 'likeable')? Translation is misleading since there is no way to render the functionally equal status of the two arguments (cf. *X likes Y* vs. *Y is good/likeable/pleasant to X*).

In other cases of double subject constructions, the primary orientation of the predicate is generally obvious, and points to the second (argument marked as a) subject. Let us take a look at three examples of Korean subject-predicate collocations:

(52)	맛이 있다	*mas.i issta*	taste.S exist	'taste good'
	땀이 나다	*ttam.i nata*	sweat.S appear	'sweat'
	낯이 두껍다	*nach.i twukkepta*	face.S thick	'be shameless'

14 Also *fit, suit, resemble, equal, contain, comprise, lack*, etc. (Greenbaum & Quirck, 1990: 345)

15 See the literature on dative subjects, or the unconventional marking of demoted subjects of psychological verbs such as *aimer, apprécier*, etc. in French (*de* N vs. *par* N).

16 'Orientation' in the sense of Lemaréchal (1998).

As a comparison between the componential reading and the translation suggests, the verb qualifies the noun component of the collocation: in *mas.i issta* 'taste good', the verb *issta* 'exist' states the existence of *mas* 'taste', just as *nata* 'appear' describes the occurrence of *ttam* 'sweat'. In *nach.i twukkepta*, regardless of the idiomatic meaning ('be brazen, shameless'), the stative verb *twukkepta* 'thick' is a property of someone's *nach* 'face', just as it would be used in its literal meaning for describing a piece of cloth or of bread. The point here is that the predicative part cannot be said to directly qualify an argument other than the one closest to the verb. Saying of a dish that '(this dish) taste exists' is not a statement that a certain dish exists, while in '(he) sweat appeared', the verb *nata* 'appear' does not assess the sudden occurrence of the human referent. This is also true of non-frozen combinations, as for instance in the most common pattern for expressing possession, e.g. in 'He.Top/S car.S exist'. The verb meaning 'to exist' is not primarily oriented toward the first subject (the possessor), but toward the second (the possessed referent). Only the existence of the second argument can be stated, negated, or questioned depending on the clause type, whereas the existence of the first subject is taken as granted. In that sense, it is the second subject which qualifies as the entity which is 'talked about', hence represents the subject in a logical sense. This goes along with selectional restrictions imposed by the predicate (as illustrated with the case of *nach.i twukkepta* 'face is thick', in which *twukkepta* is a property attributed to inanimate referents), so that it also bears the thematic role with respect to the verb.

Yet, this status conflicts with other formal properties, such as honorific agreement, that are credited to the first subject. See for instance:

(53) 차가 없으세요?
cha.ka eps.u.sey.yo
car.S not_exist.Link.Hon.TS
"Don't you/doesn't he have a car?"

(54) 땀이 나셨어요?
ttam.i na.sy.ess.e.yo
sweat.S appear.Hon.Lnk.TS
"Did you/he sweat?"

In these two short sentences, there is no first subject expressed although, as appears in the translation, both sentences refer to someone (a second or third person, possibly more than one person). This is a very common and natural mode of expression in Korean. A hint of the person referred to is formally marked by the use of allomorphs of the honorific marker *-si* on the verb. This use would be infelicitous if it could not be related to a human referent of a status higher than the speaker's (or if this status is unknown, as for a first encounter). In other terms, this marker can only be related to an unexpressed topic which, in another syntactic or interactional context (embedded clause, or reply to a question focalizing on the identity of the human referent), could be marked as a subject.[17] The property of controlling honorific agreement is, again, on the side of the first (explicit or implicit) subject.

Subject properties are thus spread on the two would-be subjects, a state of affairs that can be summarized as follows:

In so-called 'double subject constructions', as a general rule, the role of logical/thematic subject is played by the second subject, while the first subject usually displays, if any, control on honorific or anaphoric agreement on the predicate.

It can be added that the first-place subject is rightly considered as the topic of the clause,[18] in the sense that it is the entity about which 'something is said', while the rhematic component is expressed by the second subject plus the verb or adjective. Such a property is properly captured by the traditional 'double subject' analysis, which considers both constituents as subjects on different levels: the second nominal is

17 The human referent could not "surface", in these two examples, as a genitive phrase controlling the honorific marker.

18 This can be seen in terms of 'permanence référentielle' (= referential permanence, cf. initial position in the clause, control of reflexives and reciprocals, co-referent ellipsis, cf. Lazard 1998).

the subject of the verb or adjective while the first nominal is the subject of the complex sequence formed by the first NP plus the verb. This approach has the advantage not to presume that the logical 'topic' –a strange topic that can be focused on[19]– is a kind of loose disjunct not bearing any sort of syntactic relation to the rest of the clause: not only does it have control properties on the main verb, but it also displays all properties of a 'micro-syntactic constituent' (see chapter 3).

4) Lexical inconsistencies

Besides divergences in construction for some subtypes of clauses, as the ones seen above, it is expected that the morphosyntactic alignment will not be consistently reflected by lexical formations, precisely because they are of lexical, not grammatical, nature. Let us first illustrate this phenomenon with English examples.

In English, the (unmarked) subject usually precedes the verb. Does this imply that any unmarked constituent preceding the verb should be regarded as a subject? Lexical formations may obscure syntactic relations to a certain extent.

In compounds such as *finger spell(ing)* or *throat sing(ing)*, the nominal constituent is preverbal and unmarked just as regular subjects are. Even though the instrument role, which is the first interpretation coming to mind from a referential point of view, is not a prototypical role for subjects, this possibility is licensed in English. This analysis can be supported by sentences such as *Her fingers spelled the name of the murderer*, and, less acceptable, ?*Her throat is singing*. Sentences in which the body part is encoded as an adjunct phrase may however sound better. Compare: *She spelled the name of the murderer with her fingers* / (?)*He is singing with his throat*. Moreover, there is an asymmetry between the two candidate subjects when both appear in preverbal position. Consider for instance the sentence *She should have finger spelled the name of the murderer*. Only the pronoun *she* has the distribution of a

19 Indeed the first subject is a topic only when it is formally marked as a topic, or rather when it is left unexpressed.

grammatical subject, since it appears before modals and/or auxiliaries. Inversion is impossible: **(Her) fingers should have she spelled* [...]. On the referential side, however, it may be proposed that the real agent, the one that actually brings forth the process described (*spell*) are the fingers themselves not the person referred to as a whole (*she*). Of course, *finger* in *finger spell(ing)* does not display properties of a regular grammatical subject: it does not trigger agreement, cannot be demoted to the object function in a corresponding passive clause, etc. This loss of properties may however be attributed to the fact that the sequence is lexicalized. Syntactic properties holding for regular verb-argument sequences do not need to apply here. In order to assess the syntactic status of the nominal part of the compound, there is no other choice but to compare lexical formations with full sentences where the nominal is attributed a given syntactic function (such as an instrument adjunct or a subject). There is however no guarantee as to the right to claim that the compound should resume the properties of the corresponding clauses.[20] This is most likely, but this stance should be considered as a default choice that makes the description easier and more economical. In addition, on the semantic/referential side, there is much indeterminacy concerning the assignment of semantic roles to the nominal elements involved in compounds. It can be useful to note, however, that the part-whole relationships often displayed in such constructions (between the first and the second nominal) allow a high degree of "referential transitivity" to apply. For instance, body parts may inherit referential properties from their human owner (e.g. their movement can be described as having the same properties of animate beings), so that they can easily be interpreted as agents rather than as instruments.

There is thus a great deal of indeterminacy as to the grammatical and semantic functions of nominals in compounds considered in isolation. The picture becomes even more complicated when compounds are considered in their paradigms. More often than not, compounds with a similar constituent structure display heterogeneous semantic structures. This is illustrated in the following chart by a random sample

20 As is explicitly claimed in some generativist studies.

of Chinese lexicalized sequences involving the verb *chū* 'go out, leave, emerge' plus a nominal.

Compound	Compositional meaning	Meaning	Putative semantic role
出院 *chū yuàn*	go_out + hospital	'leave hospital'	SOURCE
出土 *chū tǔ*	go_out + earth	'be unearthed, dig up'	SOURCE
出国 *chū guó*	go_out + country	'go abroad'	SOURCE
出海 *chū hǎi*	go_out + sea	'go/take the sea; put to sea; launch forth'	DIRECTION
出马 *chū mǎ*	go_out + horse	'set out on a campaign; stand for election'	THEME
出兵 *chū bīng*	go_out + soldier	'send troops'	THEME
出汗 *chū hàn*	go_out + sweat	'sweat'	THEME
出力 *chū lì*	go_out + strength	'exert oneself'	THEME
出色 *chū sè*	go_out + color	'outstanding, remarkable'	THEME
出名 *chū míng*	go_out + name	'well known, famous'	THEME

As can be seen, the postposed nominal is liable to a local interpretation (ablative as in *chūguó* 'leave (one's) country', or allative as in *chūhǎi* 'leave for the sea'), or a theme role, examples of which are also liable to a causative gloss: *chūmǎ* 'bring out horses', *chūlì* '(make one's) strength go out', *chūhàn* '(let one's) sweat go out'.

Note that *chūmíng* 'go out-name = famous' is considered a Verb-Object compound in Li & Thompson's grammar (1981: 166) as would probably be *chūlì*, *chūsè* and *chūhàn*. For these examples, a subject interpretation of the second position nominal cannot be ruled out. The reasons are twofold: (1) *chū* licenses second position subjects in non frozen sentences; (2) it is the postverbal nominal that is primarily affected, literally or metaphorically, by the movement described by *chū* 'go out': sweat, strength, color, and name 'go out' rather than their human possessor (compare with *chūguó* or *chūhǎi*).

3. Loci for subjects in SPC

Having mentioned some of the difficulties in assessing the subject status for some constructions in Asian languages, what would then be the main loci for subjects in collocational sequences?

In the introductory chapter, the issue was raised whether subjects can enter frozen lexical combinations, and the generally accepted answer to this question was either negative, or positive but highly constrained. In other terms, the subject function was the least expected of syntactic functions to combine with a predicate to form a compound or a collocation. Since the perspective was that of European languages, the term 'subject' is to be understood in the frame of accusative-type languages. From a contrastive perspective, it follows that the most interesting targets for this study are subjects or equivalents of subjects according to an ideal accusative type, that is either the sole arguments of intransitive verbs (including adjectives) or the most agentive arguments of transitive verbs, irrespective of the genuine alignment type of the language in consideration.

Bearing in mind that the following classification is not necessarily justified, on formal grounds, for a specific language, it will be nevertheless helpful to distinguish three main sets of data according to the category of the predicate: (i) descriptive intransitive verbs or adjectives, (ii) other intransitive verbs, (iii) transitive verbs.

(i) descriptive intransitive verbs (or adjectives)

A great number of SPC are found with descriptive intransitive verbs or adjectives. A subclass of these, probably the first in terms of numerical importance, involves an adjective qualifying a body part whose possessor may or may not be expressed (see above double subject constructions). The body part may occasionally refer to some external possessor, as in Korean *nach.i selta* 'face.S unripe = (someone else's) face is unfamiliar'. In most cases, however, the body part is referentially linked to the potential first subject (e.g. X *nach.i twukkepta* '(lit.) X's face is thick = X is shameless'). In both examples, the subject in terms of selectional constraints is easy to determine: it is the noun referring to the body part.

There are specific cases in which the human possessor as well as the body part could, semantically speaking, qualify for the subject status. This pattern is illustrated by sequences such as Michael^belly^hungry, that can be glossed either as 'Michael is hungry (in his belly)' or '(his) belly is hungry'. The adjective can be thought of as a human quality referring to the possessor, yet the body part is the most directly involved in the state referred to. Both nouns in such examples would be morphologically marked as subjects in Korean or Japanese, or placed in preverbal position in Chinese. They are doubtlessly instances of the double subject pattern.

In some mainland South East Asian languages however, as well as in Chinese, the noun referring to the body part may occasionally or regularly be placed after the verb, in the position of an object or a locative phrase. These cases are worth taking into account, from the perspective of areal linguistics but also for structural reasons (see 2, this chapter, p. 77).

(ii) other intransitive verbs

This group includes all instances of intransitive predicates that are not adjectives or adjective-like. In other terms, stative verbs that are not gradable (although the SPC they belong to may be gradable, see Korean *caymi.issta* 'interest.exist = be interesting, funny'). They may give support verb constructions, as Kor. *yenlak.i ota* 'call.S come = get a call', or various sequences describing stative or active events, human properties as well as meteorological phenomena.

Active intransitive verbs can often be interpreted as "hidden causatives", as in the Chinese examples seen above (e.g., '(make) go_out sweat = sweat').

Besides (semantically) unaccusative verbs, other verbs, presumably unergative, are also mentioned, e.g. in Chinese:

> "An examination of the subject-predicate compound yields the observation that the predicate constituent is in most cases an adjectival verb. Only a few cases of action verbs serving as the predicate constituent can be found: for example, in *bīng-biàn* 'soldier-rebel = to mutiny, *biàn* is an action verb; in *qì-chuǎn* 'breath-pant = have asthma', *chuǎn* is an action verb; in *dì-zhèn* 'earth-quake = to have an

earthquake', *zhèn* is an action verb." (Li & Thompson, 1989: 72)

In Japanese, contrary to Shibatani's expectations[21](1990: 241), the verb *hashiru* 'run' can also enter a compound,[22] though less surprisingly with an inanimate subject, as in 口走る *kuchi-bashiru* 'mouth-run = blurt out, blab' (Irwin 2009: 4).

(iii) transitive verbs

As Shibatani (1990: 241) carefully noted about Japanese nominal compounds, "nominals corresponding to the subjects of transitive verbs are lacking, though there are some sporadic forms violating this general pattern, e.g. *musi-kui* (bug-eating) 'eating by a moth'." But Japanese is not alone in allowing the verb 'eat' to combine with a subject and yield a frozen sequence. Korean has two sequences paralleling Jap. 虫食い *mushi-kui*, i.e. 벌레먹다 *pelley-mekta* 'bug+eat' and 좀먹다 *com-mekta* 'moth+eat = worm/moth-eat(en)'.[23] These are predicative collocations that can be used either in adnominal clauses or as the main predicate of a clause. There are also a series of idiomatic sequences combining *mekta* 'eat' with, for instance, 'make up', 'ink', or 'money'. The meaning is then close to that of 들다 *tulta* 'enter'. In all these uses, *mekta* cannot take an object as a second argument, and except for the first sequences, in which 'eat' obviously retains its meaning, the verb is semantically intransitive.

(55) 좀먹은 책 / 벌레먹은 이
com-mek.un chayk / pelley-mek.un i
moth-eat.Adn book / bug-eat.Adn tooth
"a moth-eaten book" / "a decayed tooth"

---

21 "Even those nominals that correspond to the subjects of intransitive verbs are of specific type; namely, they are patients rather than agents. That is, while forms like *ame-huri* 'rain-falling' and *kata-kori* 'shoulder-stiffening' abound, we do not find compounds like **kodomo-naki* 'child-crying' and **uma-hasiri* 'horse-running'." See also Mithun (1984: 863) on incorporation: "A V like 'run' is unlikely to incorporate because its single argument is an agent."

22 In this case displaying sequential voicing (cf. 2.1)).

23 See also Mongolian зэв идэх *zev ideh* 'rust + eat = rust, corrode'.

옷에 좀이 먹었다.
os.ey com.i mek.ess.ta
cloth.Loc moth.S eat.Past.TS
"a garment is moth-eaten"

(56) 화장이 잘 먹는다.
hwacang.i cal mek.nun.ta
make-up.S well eat.Pres.TS
"The makeup blends well."

(57) 돈이 많이 먹는다
ton.i manhi mek.nun.ta
money.S a_lot eat.Pres.TS
"It is costly, expensive."

(58) 그는 귀가 아주 먹었다
ku.nun kwi.ka acwu mek.ess.ta
He.Top ear.S very eat.Past.TS
"He is stone-deaf."

In the last example (58), the exact interpretation of *mekta* in *kwi.ka mekessta* (literally 'ear.S ate = deaf') is unclear. As pointed out by Kim C.S. (pers. comm.), it could be reasonably related to the transitive verb *makta* 'obturate, obstruct'.[24] The "digestive" interpretation does not however seem totally unlikely, if one considers that being deaf is equivalent to 'eat (someone else's) words'.[25] Conversely, 'to stammer' or 'stutter' is conceived as '(one's mouth) eating (one's own words)' in Chinese (口吃 *kǒuchī* 'mouth+eat', Yip 2000: 160). Such examples are however seemingly rare.

---

24 [a] and [e] are actually alternant vowels in the remnant processes of vowel harmony. The alternation can still be observed in some verbal suffixes (e.g. the past suffixes *–ass* and *–ess* in respectively *cap.ass-* 'took' and *cwu.ess-* 'gave'), but also in ideophones and colour terms, e.g. *haymalkahta* vs. *huymelkehta* 'glossy white' (Sohn H.M. 1999: 185). There could thus have been an alternation *makta* ~ *mekta* in the history of Korean.

25 One can also consider the fact that contrary to *makta* 'obstruct', *mekta* 'eat' is already attested with several other intransitive and metaphorical uses.

(iv) subjects excluded from this study

Lastly, there is a fourth category of potential subjects that will not be considered here.

The lexicons of Korean and Japanese have retained many Sino-Korean or Sino-Japanese complex words that take on Chinese patterns.[26] As can be seen from the following chart, they can be analyzed as Verb-Subject sequences (Japanese examples are taken from Iwasaki (2002: 74-75), Korean equivalents have been added):

Sino-Japanese word		Sino-Korean word		Meaning
落葉	*raku-yoo*	落葉	*nak-yep*	'fall-leaf = falling leaves'
出火	*shuk-ka*	出火	*chwul-hwa*	'erupt-fire = outbreak of fire'
日没	*nitchi-botsu*	日沒	*il-mol*	'sun-sink = sunset'

Given that the constituents of these compounds never occur in isolation (even as an allomorphic variant), these compounds will not be considered. The sequences to be retained should involve at least one (elsewhere) free variant, such as in Kor. *kep-nata* 'fear-appear = fear' or *ceymi-issta* 'interest-exist = be interesting'.

It is indeed necessary to make a distinction between complex words and compounds.

Before investigating compound properties, focusing again on Asian languages and on subject predicate sequences, let us add a few observations on word order variations characteristic of the SEAn expressions, so as to raise again the issue of the subject status of the noun constituent.

26 Which does not mean that they are borrowed from Chinese. Many Sino-Korean and Sino-Japanese words were coined in Korea and Japan, and some were later even borrowed by Chinese.

2

Syntactic reversibility in Chinese and SEAn languages

The usual word order found in SEAn languages for SPC is of the type illustrated in the following Vietnamese example:

(59) *X đẹp người.*
X beautiful body
'X is beautiful'

A stative/adjectival verb is in close association with a body-part term, according to the following formula (Clark, 1996: 549):

(60) Human ^ Stative_verb ^ Body-Part
= "Subject has condition described by a verb located in that body part (of Subject)" (Clark 1996: 535)

Note that in attributive constructions, descriptive attributes follow the head noun. This order also occurs in SPC (Clark, 1996: 560):

(61) Human ^ Body-Part ^ Stative_verb

This case of 'syntactic reversibility' Matisoff (1986: 35) happens in Thai and Hmong. Illustrations can be found in Matisoff's works, as well as in Iwasaki (2002, 2005). Among these, many reversible expressions involving the word for "heart" are symmetrical (i.e. the same two elements may appear in two different orders) and display a semantic differenciation between a temporary state of mind and a permanent quality:

(62)	Pred. ^ *heart*	ร้อน-ใจ *róon cay*	'hot heart = feel worried'
	[± temporary state of mind]	ดี-ใจ *dii cay*	'good heart = glad'
	heart ^ Pred.	ใจ-ร้อน *cay róon*	'heart hot = short-tempered'
	[± permanent quality]	ใจ-ดี *cay dii*	'heart good = kind'

According to Jaisser (1990: 175), the same syntactic phenomenon holds for Hmong, with sometimes a semantic difference as in Thai, but this is far from being systematic.

Both orders also appear in Vietnamese, and Clark (1996: 561) states that it depends on the origin of the sequence: "[...] Sino-Vietnamese compounds take the Chinese word order of descriptive modification preceding the head noun, as opposed to the Vietnamese order of postposed descriptive modification." This remark can be exemplified in (63a) with the expression 'gall afraid' (cf. Chinese *dǎn-qiè*, same meaning), whereas 'big liver' displays in (63b) a reverse order of constituents. The same observation applies in (64a~b):

(63) (a) Vi: *đảm-khiếp* 'gall afraid = cowardly'[27]
(b) Vi: *to gan* 'big liver[28] = bold, daring'

(64) (a) *mắt đui* 'eye blind = blind' (derogatory)
(b) *mù mắt* 'blind eye = blind' (neutral)

There are however cases of syntactic variation irrespective of the origin of the components. In the following example, the same words can take on both orders. Only the order Adjective + Body part allows a metaphorical interpretation ('lazy'):

27 Cf. Ch: 胆怯 *dǎn-qiè* gallbladder-frightened 'cowardly'.
28 SV term for 'liver' is *can; gan* also means 'courageous, brave, tough'.

(65) (a) *dài lưng* 'long[29] back = lazy, idle' (metaphorical)
(b) *lưng dài* 'back long = have a long back' (literal)

The order descriptive verb ^ body part is probably basic for noun-predicate sequences involving a body part. For instance, this word order is used when expressing that some body part hurts:

(66) *đau mình* 'ache body'
đau đầu 'ache head'

This second position is however not considered a subject position in Vietnamese. Basic word order is SVO, and the postverbal position is said to host objects or locative complements. Indeed, as a general rule, researchers working on SEAn languages seem to consider the body part in second position as a locative phrase. Consider the following glosses from Clark:

(67) Lan ^ be hungry ^ stomach 'Lan is hungry in the stomach'
Youa ^ be lonely ^ liver 'Youa is lonely in the liver: homesick'
Arunee ^ be good ^ heart 'Arunee is happy (in the heart)'

From a semantic-referential perspective, the postverbal argument can be interpreted as a subject if one considers that it is the body part, in the first place, that is affected by the process, before, transitively, it applies to the possessor.[30] It is also not unusual to find the distinction between subjects and locative complements blurred in other cases. For instance, the possessor in possessive constructions can be marked as a locative complement in NEA languages ('to X Y(.S) exists'[31]), and,

---

29 *dái* = long.

30 It is not claimed here that these second-position nouns should be considered as subjects because they may correspond to morphologically marked subjects in NEAn languages (Korean, Japanese, and Mongolian); such a claim would be arbitrary. Nevertheless, it can be safely claimed that second-position arguments in SEAn languages may play the same functional role as do morphological subjects in NEAn languages.

31 As with the Japanese addressee-locative marking particle *–ni* or Mongolian *–d/–t* (but Korean makes a distinction between human and non-human locations).

indeed, referentially serves as a sort of 'animate location'. Conversely, the possessee itself is encoded as a subject in NEAn languages. In this case, it corresponds to a second-position argument in SEAn languages:

(68)	Ch:	他	有	很多	朋友
		Tā	***yǒu***	*hěn duō*	*péngyou.*
	Vi:	*Nó*	***có***	*nhiều*	*bạn.*
		3P	have	much, many	friend
	Th:	เขา	มี	เพื่อน	มาก
		kháw	***mii***	*phûan*	*yàng.*
		3P	have	friend	much, many

"He has many friends."

Verbs translated here by 'have' also enter existential constructions where they are presumably intransitive (except if one considers that there is an unrecoverable 'universal' possessor):[32]

(69)	Ch:	有	一个	酒吧
		yǒu	*yī ge*	*jiǔ bā*
		be	one NumCl	bar
	Vi:	***Có***	*một*	*quán rượu*
		be	one	bar
	Th:	มี		บาร์
		mii		*baa*
		be		bar

"There is a bar."

In these cases, the sole argument, hence presumably a subject, is again in second position. The description would get a lot simpler if one assumed that Ch. *yǒu*, Th. *mii*, Vi. *có* are always intransitive verbs, and,

32 Comparing *yǒu*-structures with animate loci or places, Li & Thompson insist that "In both types of examples, something is being claimed to exist; the difference is whether it is said to exist with respect to a place or to another entity. In fact, for some Mandarin sentences with *yǒu* 'exist', either a 'have' or a 'there is' translation is appropriate." (Li & Thompson, 1981: 513)

for instance, that the possessor in possessive clauses is an unmarked locative complement, as opposed to places. Places may also be fronted, in which case they are optionally marked as locative phrases, e.g. in Chinese (Li & Thompson 1981: 510-511, Zhang 2011):

(70) Ch: 在院子里有一只狗
(zài) yuànzi li yǒu yi zhī gǒu.
(at) yard in exist one NumCl dog
"There's a dog in the yard.", or:
yǒu yi zhī gǒu zài yuànzi li.
exist one NumCl dog at yard in

Otherwise, it could be considered that both the possessor and the possessee are subjects. In this latter hypothesis, the possessee could be analyzed as the sole argument and subject of *exist* (as a VP-internal subject), while the possessor would be the subject of the complex sequence *friend-exist*. This is the traditional way of analyzing double-subject constructions in Korean and Japanese, as well as in Chinese when both would-be subjects are preposed. This analysis may equally apply to structures involving an intransitive verb where one would-be subject is preposed and the other is postposed, as long as one considers that postposed subjects are licensed.

Now, assuming the previously mentioned phenomenon of 'syntactic reversibility', it appears that contrasting the word order of equivalent sequences in structurally similar languages does not gives hints as to whether a given word order should be more natural or basic for a given combination of constituents. In the following chart, four samples involving the same elements (with the exception of Ch. *lǎn gǔtóu* 'lazy bone' instead of 'back-long' in the other languages) are contrasted in Chinese, Vietnamese and Thai. Sequences that are assumed to follow the basic word order of these languages (i.e. SV) appear in grey. As can be seen, each single sequence can be encoded differently in at least one language. Moreover, it cannot be said that there is a correlation between the non-basic order and the extent of possible paradigmatic variation in the subject position. 'head-ache' sentences are sentences in which the noun position is most open to paradigmatic variation (since several body parts other than one's head can ache); they however display a VS order in Vietnamese and Thai, yet the Vietnamese sequence 'back long' in its idiomatic meaning ("lazy") follows a perfectly regular SV order (remember VS 'long back' seen above in a literal sense).

	Weather-clause	*Ache*-clause	*Deaf*-clause	*Lazy*-clause
Chinese	刮风/風 *guā fēng* blow wind	头痛 *tóu tòng* head ache	耳聋 *ěr lóng* ear deaf	懒骨头 *lǎn gǔtóu* lazy bone 骨头懒 *gǔtóu lǎn* bone lazy
Vietnamese	*gió thổi* wind blow	*đau đầu* ache head	*điếc tái* deaf ear	*lưng dài* back long
Thai	ลม-พัด *lohm phát* wind blow	ปวด-หัว *pùat hŭa* painful head	หู-หนวก *hŭu nùak* ear deaf	สันหลัง-ยาว *lăŋ yaaw* back long

There is no doubt that the noun 'wind' is the logical subject in the 'wind-blow' or 'blow-wind' sequences. In other term, 'wind' is the only possible constituent of which one can say that it blows. In the case of 'back long', even though the possessor of the back could also be said to be long, this would be a misinterpretation. The locative interpretation too is not appropriate in both cases (**(It) blows in the wind / *X is long in the back*). As these sequences follow the usual SV order in Vietnamese and Thai, the mapping between the logical subject and the syntactic subject can be claimed to be consistent, but it would not be the case in Chinese *guā fēng* 'blow wind'.

In the case of 'head-painful/ache', it can be said that the aching of a head implies the aching of its possessor as well, so that the status of logical subject is shared by both the head and the human being involved, and variation could be expected for *ache*-clauses. Yet Thai could also be claimed not to be consistent in treating a painful head and a deaf ear differently, because it is even clearer that the deafness of one's ears –in this case, not only one ear is involved– implies that of the possessor.

If we now take a closer look at Chinese data, it appears that Chinese allows a great deal of word-order variation as for the respective position of subjects and verbs (or adjectives) in SPC.[33] The following data were elicited thanks to a Chinese informant and friend, Zhang C.G. In the chart, a double line sets idiomatic and transparent collocations apart:

(71)	Meaning	Noun – Predicate order	Predicate – Noun Order
xīn hēi	'heart-black = black-hearted'	✓他心黑	✓他黑心
shǒu kuài	'hand-quick = agile'	✓他手快	✓他快手
liǎnpí hòu	'face-thin = shameless'	✓他脸皮厚	✓他厚脸皮
dǎn dà	'gall-big = brave'	✓他胆大	✓他大胆
dǎn xiǎo	'gall-small = cowardly'	✓他胆小	✓他小胆
nián qīng	'age-light = young'	✓他年轻	✓他轻年
gǔtóu lǎn	'bone-lazy = lazy'	✓他骨头懒	✓他懒骨头
gèr dà	'body-big = big'	✓他个儿大	*他大个儿
gèr gāo	'body-tall = tall'	✓他个儿高	*他高个儿
nián lǎo	'year-old = old (over 60)'	✓他年老	*他老年
nián mài	'year-aged = old (over 70)'	✓他年迈	*他迈年
yǎn(jing) xiā	'eye-blind = blind'	✓他眼(睛)瞎	✓他瞎眼(睛)
ěr(dǔo) lóng	'ear-deaf = deaf'	✓他耳(朵)聋	(✓)他聋耳(朵)
kǒu kě	'mouth-thirsty = thirsty'	✓他口渴	*他渴口
dùzi è	'belly-hungry = hungry'	✓他肚子饿	(✓)他饿肚子
shēntǐ pàng	'body-fat = fat'	✓他身体(很)胖	*他胖身体

Note that V+N or Adj+N sequences (rightmost column) cannot be analyzed as nominal predicates, formed out of a noun modified by an

33 To my knowledge, the phenomenon of 'syntactic reversibility' in Chinese SPC is not recorded in the literature.

attributive verb. If this was the case, the copula *shì* would be needed, but the complex predicate functions just like an adjectival verb. Both V(/Adj) N and NV(/Adj) sequences are best described as synthetic collocations. The exact syntactic function of the nominal argument can however be an issue. Let us suppose first a locative interpretation. Whether the noun comes after or before the verb, there is no possibility of inserting a spatial marker such as *zài* "in", like in **tā kuài zài shǒu* /**zài shǒu tā kuài* 'He is quick in (his) hand(s)', or **tā è zài dùzi*/**zài dùzi tā è* 'He is hungry in (his) belly'. The subject interpretation is actually more convincing since: (i) at least for idiomatic sequences displayed in the upper part of the chart, it is the body part that is qualified by the verb, not the human possessor; (ii), it is a property of *some* subjects to be allowed either as preposed or postposed without any additional (e.g. prepositional) marking (see ex. 27-32). As a matter of fact, subjects referring to body parts in SPC share properties with other types of subjects that can be postposed.

Subject nouns that can be postposed are essentially non topical with respect to their predicate. A prototypical example is the meteorological clause 'blow-wind'. Without further specification, the wind is so closely associated with the event of blowing that the occurrence of the event conditions the existence of the entity, and conversely. In other terms, if there is no blowing, there is no wind, if there is wind, it cannot but blow. By extension, all predicates that describe the appearance or disappearance of an entity (including *come, be born, die*, etc.) intrinsically give the entity they are predicated of an equal informational load: both the verb and the entity are equally rhematic. This is however only a default interpretation that can be cancelled if needed.

Subjects involved in the SPC illustrated above are mostly relational nouns describing body parts, and in this respect, they are closely associated (by a metonymic relationship) to their possessor. It does not matter whether the possessor is explicitly mentioned or not, a body part is intrinsically anaphoric, i.e., not topical, by nature. It is thus no surprise that they may be postposed as well.

As will be mentioned in chapter 3, SPC can also be described, in Halliday's terms, as entertaining a relationship of mutual expectancy between the noun and the verb, so that there is a close link that associates the body part and the qualifying predicate.[34]

This may account for the non regularity of the relative order of nouns and verbs in SPC. It appears however that transparent and redundant SPC of the 'age-old' type tendencially disallow their noun constituent to be postposed. For instance, the sequence *gèr gāo* 'body-tall = tall', together with most SPC of the lower part of the chart, does not license an 'inverted' order (**gāo gèr*).

To sum up, the subject status of the nominal element in South East Asian and in Chinese SPC may be debatable given that the noun can occur in a non-prototypical subject position, namely after the verb. A locative interpretation has however three main apparent shortcomings. Firstly, the noun constituent cannot take a locative marker as locative complements usually do in these languages. Secondly, when it is preposed, it does not occur in a topical position, but between the topic (e.g. the human possessor) and the verb. Again, these problems can be accounted for by the collocational nature of the sequence. This can be demonstrated by the paradigmatic frozenness of the sequence, which lets one expect an irregular syntactic behavior. The third shortcoming constitutes a more serious counterargument to the locative analysis: in the case of idiomatic sequences, the predicate clearly describes a property of the body part, not of another constituent, and specifically not of the possessor. In a locative interpretation, Chinese VN combinations "He (is) light-age" "He (is) thin-gall" should be read respectively as "He (is) light in his age" and "He (is) thin in his gall". These glosses are acceptable only if the complement is not optional, because the sentences cannot mean "He (is) light" or "He (is) thin". An obligatory locative complement should thus be included in the valence frame of the verb, but only in the

34 This can be thought of as a hint of their wordhood, but it has more to do with the linguistic organization of a given language than with an essential referential link between the entity and the event referred to. This wordhood can in turn be called upon to justify the fact that the noun constituent cannot be expected to have a regular syntactic behavior. Due to the collocational nature of the sequence, it is illusory to think that the subject constituent should display regular subject characteristics, neither in transformational (e.g. passive formation) nor in positional terms. Such subjects are not free-choice constituents, so that even though they can be considered as the logical/referential subjects, they do not pertain to syntax in its most usual definition (see Chap. 3).

context of collocations. Such a description would be an *ad hoc* as well as an expensive one.

On the other hand, considering that the noun is, independently of its position, a subject, is supported by the facts (i) that the verb can be described as an intransitive verb that does not need any additional complement, (ii) that the noun is qualified by the predicate as is any regular subject, and (iii), that subjects, when they are non-topical, can be postposed.

Remember that in SOV languages such as Korean or Japanese, the noun component of similar combinations would be marked as a rhematic subject rather than as a topic, and would never get a locative marker. The difference in structure with respect to South East Asian languages implies different ways of dealing with a non-topical subject, but the mechanism is essentially the same. That being said, whatever the position or morphological marking of the noun is, its subject status is not that of a 'micro-syntactic constituent', i.e. it is not a free choice argument.

Let us now consider criteria for frozenness in Asian languages.

3

Illustration of compound properties in Asian languages

Among sequences that can be as considered frozen for any reason, compound words are not the most cohesive ones. In this respect they can be opposed to complex words formed by lexical or grammatical derivation. For instance, Turkish vowel harmony applies to suffixes, not to compounds. Thus, the famous Turkish plural suffix has the front vowel [e] in *kibrit-ler* 'matches', while it has the back vowel [a] in *karpuz-lar* 'watermelons'. Vowel agreement, though, does not apply to compound words such as *bin-başı* [thousand-head] '(army) major' (Haspelmath 2002: 157). As noted by Haspelmath (2002: 157), the Siberian language Chukchee, another language with vowel harmony, is atypical in having vowel harmony applying to compound words as well: a word like *kupre-n* 'net' changes to *kopra-* in *pəlvəntə-kopra-n* 'metal net'. Mongolian behaves like Turkish. When a suffix is added to a word stem, the vowel of the suffix is usually chosen out of four possibilities ([a, o, e, ö]), and should never belong to the set of (originally) back vowels (i.e. [a, o, u]) if the stem word contains (originally) front vowels (i.e. [e, ö, ü]), or conversely should not display front vowels if its base has back vowels. Thus, the adjective-derivative suffix *–l(a)g* in the following examples (Kullmann 1996: 50) complies with the stem vowel:

мах *mah*	'meat'	мах-лаг *mah-lag*	'fleshy, fat'
тос *tos*	'oil'	тос-лог *tos-log*	'oily'
үс *üs*	'harmony'	үс-лэг *üs-leg*	'harmonious, polite'
хөлөнгө *hölöngö*	'wealth'	хөлөнгө-лөг *hölöngö-lög*	'wealthy'

Typically though, no such rules apply when full words are combined together, as illustrated in усан үзэм *usan üzem* 'water raisin = grapes', үхэр буу *üher buu* 'cow gun = cannon', or төмөр зам *tömör zam* 'iron road = railway' (Kuiimann 1996: 58).

This difference of behavior between affixes and words, is expected also in terms of syntactic cohesion: affixes, whether word-formative or grammatical, should not be separated from the word they attach to (except by other affixes). This is precisely part of their definition. Words in compounds, on the other hand, usually show less syntactic cohesion, and again, there is a difference between different subtypes of compounds.

Predicative compounds are in general less cohesive than other types of compounds. This can be illustrated with Chinese tonal neutralization. In Mandarin Chinese, contrary to other Sinitic languages such as Cantonese, tonal neutralization may occur on unstressed or weak syllables such as grammatical bound morphemes (e.g. the genitive particle *de*, the aspect marker *le*, etc.). The neutral tone is perceived as comparatively short, generally at mid-height, but its exact tone value varies according to the tone of the preceding syllable (Cheng 1973, Chen 1984, Packard 1998b). Tone neutralization may as well occur on the second syllable of dissyllabic words, because the second syllable tends to be unstressed. In pinyin transcription, the neutral tone is left unmarked. Examples include: 谢谢 *xièxie* 'thank + thank = thanks', 买卖 *mǎimai* 'trade, business' (vs. *mǎi mài* 'buy + sell = buy and sell', 东西 *dōngxi* 'thing; object' (vs. *dōng xī* 'east + west = east and west') (Hsu 2002: 27-28). Neutralization may vary greatly among speakers, but in any case, Chi (1985: 74, quoted in Packard 2000: 112), claims that it does not affect most Verb-Object compounds. Similarly, Subject-Predicate collocations in Mandarin Chinese do not seem to display tone neutralization.

1. Sandhi phenomena and suprasegmental integration in Japanese

The phonological cohesion of a complex sequence is often taken as a good indication of its wordhood. It can take various forms:

suprasegmental when it involves the tonal or accentual pattern of the sequence, or segmental when it modifies the segmental part (i.e. single vowels or consonants). Both cases are best illustrated with Japanese since this language displays clear phonological hints of integration for Subject-Predicate sequences. One of them is the sandhi phenomenon, known as 連濁 *rendaku* ('sequential voicing'). It is illustrated below in the SPC *ki-zuku* '*ki*-attach = pay attention to':

(72) 恋しちゃったんだ // 多分 気づいてないでしょう?
koishi.chat.ta.n.da // tabun ki-zui.te nai desh.ou?
love.finish.Past.Nm.Cop // maybe ki.attach.Con Neg Cop.TS
"I've fallen in love with you // Maybe you don't know that?"
(Yui, *Che.r.ry*)

Rendaku may apply to the second word in a complex sequence if it begins with a voiceless consonant that has a (phonological) voiced counterpart. When rendaku applies, the initial consonants [k, t, s, h] are sonorized to [g, d, z, b], as in 小太鼓 *kodaiko* 'small drum', from *ko* 'small' and *taiko* 'drum', or 朝風呂 *asaburo* 'morning bath', from *asa* 'morning' and *furo* 'bath'. It is however constrained by the so-called Lyman's law (Lyman 1894, previously stated by Motoori 1822), a law of dissimilation which postulates that rendaku does not apply when the second word already contains a sounded obstruent (濁音 *dakuon*). Thus, the 'divine wind', a series of typhoons that protected the Japanese during the Mongolian invasions of 1274 and 1281, is spelled 神風 *kamikaze* (from *kami* 'god' and *kaze* 'wind') instead of **kamigaze*, because of the [z] sound in the second word. Several further constraints have been proposed, such as the lexical type of the compound (*rendaku* does not normally apply in copulative compounds), the origin of the lexemes (*rendaku* appears with lower frequency in Sino-Japanese words, and almost never in modern foreign loanwords), etc., but some cases are still difficult to explain, except in terms of lexical properties of individual words (see the names of the two indigenous syllabaries, 平仮名 *hira-**g**ana* vs. 片仮名 ***k**ata-kana*, Kubozono 2005: 5).

Naturally, this process only shows up in compounds, and never in sequences interrupted by a particle, as illustrated in the following with the subject particle *ga*[35] or the genitive particle *no*:

(73) 腹が黒い
hara.ga ***k**uroi*. (**guroi* vs. *hara-**g**uroi*)
belly.S black
'be black-hearted'
桃の木
momo no ki (**gi*)
peach Gen tree
'peach tree'

Rendaku however occurs with high frequency in various synthetic compounds when proper phonological conditions are met, as illustrated in the following charts (cf. Shibatani 1990: 237-238; Iwasaki, 2002: 74-75):

-Object-verb substantive compounds:

kan 'can'	+ *kir(u)* 'cut'	→ カンきり	*kan-kiri*	'can-opener'
hito 'person'	+ ***k**oros(u)* 'kill'	→ 人殺し	*hito-**g**oroshi*	'murder(er)'[36]

-Object-verb predicative compounds:

koshi 'waist'	+ *kake(ru)* 'hang'	→ 腰掛ける	*kosi-kake(ru)*	'sit down'
na 'name'	+ ***ts**uke(ru)* 'make'	→ 名付ける	*na-zuke(ru)*	'name'

-Subject-verb/adjective substantive compounds:

ame 'rain'	+ *fur(ru)* 'fall'	→ 雨降り	*ame-furi*	'rainfall'
yuki 'snow'	+ ***d**oke(ru)* 'melt'	→ 雪解け	*yuki-**d**oke*	'snow-melting'

35 The sequence retains its idiomatic meaning.

36 *hito-goroshi* belongs to a set of words that were previously recorded without rendaku (see the form *fito-coroxi* in the *Vocabulario da lingoa de Iapam* by J. Rodriguez (1603)). On diachronic changes in sequential voicing, see Hibiya (draft, n.d.). On the influence of semantic factors, see Suzuki (2008).

-Subject-verb/adjective predicative compounds:

kokochi 'feeling'	+ *yoi* 'good'	→ 心地よい	*kokochi-yoi*	'comfortable'
haba 'width'	+ *__h__iroi* 'wide'	→ 幅拾い	*haba-__b__iroi*	'wide'

There are many other instances of Subject-Predicate predicative compounds displaying *rendaku*, cf. 気付く *ki-zuku* 'ki, spirit + turn on = notice', 泡立つ *awa-datsu* 'bubble + stand = foam', 色ずく *iro-zuku* 'color + attach = get colored', 名高い *na-dakai* 'noun + big = famous', etc.

Another hint for phonological integration can be found in the tonal pattern of word combinations. In Standard Japanese (as spoken in Tokyo), basic words forbid an interrupted succession of syllables with high tones (here symbolized as H^n). This constraint holds for simple words such as 心 /ko^{ko}ro/ 'heart' (LHL) or 桜 /sa^{kura}/ 'cherry' (LHH). Putative sequences such as /^{ko}ko^{ro}/ or /^{sa}ku^{ra}/ would be ruled out. Noun-Noun compounds also comply with this rule (e.g. 色紙 /i^{ro}gami/ 'color paper' (LHLL)), as do Subject-Predicate compounds:

Noun tonal pattern	Pred. tonal pattern	Putative output	Actual output
/a^{wa}/ 'bubble'	/^{ta}tsu/ 'stand up'	/a^{wada}tsu/	/a^{wada}tsu/ (泡立つ) 'foam'
/ha^{ra}/ 'belly'	/ku^{ro}i/ 'black'	*/ha^{ra}gu^{ro}i/	/ha^{raguro}i/ (腹が黒い) 'black-hearted, evil'
/mi^{mi}/ 'ear'	/sa^{to}i/ 'smart, sharp'	*/mi^{mi}za^{to}i/	/mi^{mizato}i/ (耳ざとい) 'quick of hearing'
/^{me}/ 'eye'	/sa^{me}ru/ 'open'	*/^{me}za^{me}ru/	/me^{zame}ru/ (目覚める) 'wake up'
/^{te}/ 'hand'	/ha^{ya}i/ 'fast'	*/^{te}ba^{ya}i/	/te^{baya}i/ (手早い) 'quick, nimble'

2. Morphological and syntactic integration

When phonological evidence lacks, the wordhood of a compound should theoretically be assessed by its morphological and/or syntactic integrity. In other terms, although components of compound are words themselves, the compound should behave like a single word. This apparently contradictory statement is resolved if one considers that the word quality of the components of a compound has to be checked in other contexts than the compound itself. Thus, each of the components should be able to function as a free word in isolation, but as a bound word inside the compound. This implies that there should be different occurrences of the same word. It is however debatable at which point those different occurrences should or should not display exactly the same phonological output. Differences related to suprasegmental features such as tone or accent are generally overlooked. Indeed, alongside other properties, a free word entering a compound may lose or change some of its phonological properties (cf. sandhi or vowel harmony phenomena mentioned above): this is is taken as a hint of integration. Problems occur when there is a loss or a radical change in the segmental integrity.

For instance, *na* in Jap. *na-dakai* 'name+big = famous', or Ch. *míng* in *chūmíng* 'emerge+name = famous' cannot occur in isolation, although they are obviously related to the corresponding free words 名前 *namae* and 名字 *míngzi*. Similarly in both languages, it is moreover the first syllable that semantically bears the main –if not the sole– semantic content (i.e. the meaning 'name'). Indeed, Jap. *mae* means 'before', and Ch. *zi* is a semantically empty pseudo-morpheme that serves as a word-formative affix (cf. 儿子 *érzi* 'son', 蚊子 *wénzi* 'mosquito', 鼻子 *bízi* 'nose', 帽子 *màozi* 'hat', 裤子 *kùzi* 'trousers', 椅子 *yǐzi* 'chair', etc., Kratochvíl, 1968: 68). In such cases, the segmental loss results only in a partial difference of the *signifiant*, not of the *signifié*. Even though the phenomena in Japanese and Chinese are slightly different, *na* and *namae* on the one hand, *míng* and *míngzi* on the other, can be considered as variants[37] of the same word.

Some segmental losses are more dramatic when a semantically heavy morpheme such as a preposition is completely left out from the

37 Thus 'allolexes' rather than 'allomorphs'. Back-clipping of complex words is a pervasive phenomenon in several Asian languages.

compound. This happens in Tibetan. In this language, compounds containing more than two syllables are "particularly liable to be clipped into disyllabic stress groups–for example, [...] *sñiñ-ÑE* < *sñiñ-dań ÑE* "be close to the heart → love," [...] *yid-ON-* < *yid-du ON-* "come into the mind → be pleasing" (Beyer 1992: 106). Such data are more problematic, but it could be said, precisely because corresponding long forms exist in isolation, that the short forms in compounds retain the same semantic characteristics as their longer counterpart. The explanation is circular, except if assumes that the link between the two forms is active in the speakers' competence.[38]

The condition of word integrity can be thus rephrased in the following terms: a word component of a compound should retain the semantic integrity and part of the phonetic output it displays in isolation. Along with the 'loss' of segments, the word is also expected to lose part of or all of its syntactic properties. For instance, Japanese *na* in *na-dakai* cannot take the subject particle *–ga*:

(74) **na.ga-dakai*
name.S-big

Two types of syntactic properties considered in studies on compounds can be distinguished in theory. The first type is linked to the syntactic, or syntagmatic, cohesion of the sequence, i.e. the problem of whether the sequence can be separated or not, and if so, by what kind of elements. The second type relates to the functional independence of each component in syntax, that is, for instance, whether it can get modifiers of its own. These two sets of syntactic properties often interfere with each other.

An ideal situation is presented by the compound verbs in Tinrin[39] discussed by Osumi (1995: 135), precisely because these are verbs "whose constituents are tied closely to each other, functioning as a single verb. These compound verbs are more internally cohesive than serial

38 This position would imply that wordhood is a neurolinguistic issue rather than a linguistic one. The same kind of problem is posed by acronyms.

39 Tinrin is an Austronesian (Melanesian) language of southern New Caledonia.

constructions. The constituents of the compound cannot be separated by any modifier, nor can either of them take an individual adjunct." Examples of SPC she gives are: *wù-si* 'belly+go = to have diarrhea'; *mee-fwidri* 'head+full = to have a cold'; *mee-mwâârrî* 'head+turn round = get drunk' (Osumi 1995: 138).

On the other extremity, a less-than-ideal situation is illustrated by Tibetan Noun-Verb synthetic 'compounds' (Beyer 1996: 106 sq.) of the following type:

(75) (i) With a 'patient-verb' relationship: *sgra-SGYUR* "change words → translate," [...] *mgo-DON* "hold up the head → be proud," *mgo-SKOR* "encircle the head → deceive," [...] *thugs-SÑUŃ* "sicken the heart → be disagreeable," *sems-GSO* "heal the mind → console," *n-ań-THUŃ* "shorten the disposition → lose one's temper," *thag-TŠAD* "cut the rope → decide."
(ii) With other kinds of relationships to the verb: *blo-s TAŃ* "dismiss WITH the mind → renounce," *lam-la KHYER* "carry ON the road → put to daily use," *sems-la SBYAR* "take TO mind → pay attention," [...] *yid-du OŃ* "come INTO the mind → be pleasing."

After presenting these examples, the author states (Beyer 1996: 131, note 8) that:

> "Despite the fact that they are compounds, such verbs can be syntactically discontinuous. The negative particle *mI-* "NOT" occurs immediately before a verbal tense stem, and thus after the noun portion of a NOUN + VERB → VERB compound–thus, for example, *mgo-KHOR* "have the head encircled → become confused" *khyed-kyi kha-sbyań-gis ńed mgo-mi-Nkhor* "We are not taken in by your eloquence." Other propositional participants can also come between the two components of such verb compounds."

In Chinese, Li & Thompson (1981: 165) show variations in the degree of syntactic or syntagmatic cohesion of Chinese Verb-Object 'compounds'. Some are considered as 'fused lexical units' that, together with a "highly idiomatic" meaning, are claimed to "no longer retain properties of the syntactic structure verb + object". Among these, some, like 担心 *dānxīn* 'bear+heart = worry', 得罪 *dézuì* 'get+offense = offend', or 注意 *zhùyì* 'pour+intention = pay attention' may further function as transitive verbs, allowing an additional object, while others (开心 *kāixīn* 'open+heart = happy', 失望 *shíwàng* 'lose+hope = be disappointed') are intransitive. Examples:

(76) 我很担心这件事
wǒ hěn dānxīn zhè jiàn shì
I very worry this NumCl matter
"I am very worried about this matter."

(77) 我很开心
wǒ hěn kāixīn
I very happy
"I am very happy."

Another group of sequences retain syntactic properties that are characteristic of free sequences. According to the same authors (Li & Thompson 1981: 166), the sequence *chūmíng* 'noun+emerge = famous', labelled as a 'verb-object compound',[40] behaves as a lexical (adjectival) unit when modified by the intensifier *hěn* 'very' or the intensifying suffix *jí* 'extremely' (ex. 78). Yet both elements of the compound can also take modifiers of their own as if it were a sequence of an independent verb and an independent noun, respectively taking on the aspect marker *le* and the adjective *dà* 'big' (ex. 79):[41]

---

40 Similar properties are discussed for *tóuténg* 'head+ache = have a headache' (Li & Thompson 1981: 70ff.).

41 Some native speakers may however reject the stative interpretation of example (78) (W. Behr, pers. comm.).

(78) 他很出名
tā hěn chūmíng
3sg very famous
"S/He is very famous."

他出名极了
tā chūmíng jí le
3sg famous extremely Part
"S/He is extremely famous."

(79) 他出了大名了?
tā chū le dà míng le
3sg emerge Perf big name Part
"S/He became very famous."

The facility with which assumed compounds in Mandarin Chinese may syntactically behave as free sequences has been assessed by many authors. For example:

> "it is somewhat difficult to place constructions like *zǒulù* (or perhaps *zǒu lù*) 'to walk' (*zǒu* 'to walk', a free morpheme, and *lù* 'road', also a free morpheme) or *chīfàn* (or perhaps *chī fàn*) 'to eat' (*chī* 'to eat', a free morpheme, and *fàn* 'cooked rice, food', also a free morpheme) on either side of the dividing line [i.e. between morphological and syntactic constructions], mainly because they behave as single words in some cases and as constructions of words in others." (Kratochvíl, 1968: 77)

Typical tests that have been used to assess the syntactic integrity of compounds include adverb insertion (i) and negation insertion between the noun and the verb. In Chinese, the placement of negation can be checked either in declarative (ii) or interrogative sentences (iii) (in 'A-not-A questions'). Again, a given Noun-Verb sequence may be treated as a word, or as a separable sequence (examples from Li & Thompson, 1981: 70-72):

(80) (i) 张三很头痛
Zhāngsān hěn tóuténg
Zhangsan very headache
"Zhangsan has a severe headache."

(ii) 张三不头痛
Zhāngsān bu tóuténg
Zhangsan Neg headache
"Zhangsan doesn't have a headache."
(iii) 张三头痛不头痛?
Zhāngsān tóuténg bu tóuténg?
Zhangsan headache Neg headache
"Does Zhangsan have a headache?"
vs.

(81) (i′) *tóu hěn téng*
head very ache
(ii′) *tóu bu téng*
head not ache
(iii′) *tóu téng bu téng*?
head ache not ache

However, according to the authors (Li & Thompson 1981: 72), only a few sequences display such labile properties (e.g. *tóuteng*, 头昏 *tóuhūn* 'head-dizzy', 眼花 *yǎnhuā* 'eye-fuzzy = fuzzy visioned'). The following list presents Subject-Predicate sequences that are assumed to be (genuine) compounds (Li & Thompson 1981: 72-73):

嘴硬	*zuǐ-yìng*	'mouth-hard	= argumentative'
眼红	*yǎn-hóng*	'eye-red	= covetous'
脸嫩	*liǎnnèn*	'face-tender	= basheful'
手紧	*shǒu-jǐn*	'hand-tight	= stingy'
手勤	*shǒu-qín*	'hand-diligent	= diligent (in manual work)'
手毒	*shoǔ-dú*	'hand-poisonous	= vicious'
心酸	*xīn-suān*	'heart-sore	= distressed'
心软	*xīn-ruǎn*	'heart-soft	= softhearted'
胆寒	*dǎn-hán*	'gall-cold	= fearful'

胆大	*dǎn-xiǎo*	'gall-small	= cowardly'
胆小	*dǎn-dà*	'gall-big	= brave'
命苦	*mìng-kǔ*	'life-bitter	= unfortunate'
性急	*xìng-jí*	'temper-anxious	= impatient'
年轻	*nián-qīng*	'age-light	= young'
声张	*shēng-zhāng*	'noise-open up	= make noise (about it)'

When two Subject-Predicate sequences have two different outputs, in syntactic as well as phonological terms, as it is the case with many Japanese SPC, syntactic environments may vary accordingly. For instance, the sequence 彼は力が強い *chikara.ga zuyoi* 'strength.S strong = strong' can function as the main predicate of an independent clause (82), or be modified by a genitive phrase (83):

(82)	ローレンス・フィッシュバーンに	やられた。	彼は	力が強いよ。[42]
	rōrensu fisshubān.ni	*yara.re.ta.*	*kare.wa*	*chikara.ga tsuyoi.yo*
	Laurence Fishburn.by	do.Pass.Past	he.Top	strength.S strong.TS

"Yes, by Laurence Fishburne. He's strong."

(83)	彼は	足の	力が	強い
	kare.wa	*ashi.no*	*chikara.ga*	*tsuyoi*
	he.Top	leg.Gen	power.S	strong

"He is strong in his legs/He has strength in his legs."

Whereas the corresponding lexical sequence with *rendaku* and no subject particle would conversely rather appear in dependent clauses such as in attributive function (*chikara-zuyoi* + N), or in complement

42 From an interview with Keanu Reeves, where he is asked whether he got kicked a lot (http://jabondy.free.fr/267Matrix/Jap/jap3.htm).

clauses:

(84) 彼は 自身が 力強いと 思って いる
kare.wa *jishin.ga* *chikara-zuyoi.to* *omot.te* *iru*
he.Top self.S strength-strong.Quot think.Con be
"I think he is strong."

(85) 私は、 彼は 力強いと 言った
watashi.wa, *kare.wa* *chikara-zuyoi.to* *it.ta*
I.Top he.Top strength-strong.Quot say.Past
"I said he is strong."

It is however not the case that all collocations undergoing *rendaku* are subject to identical syntactic constraints. For instance *mimi-zatoi* 'ear-clever/sharp = have sharp ears' can appear as the main predicate of an independent sentence (e.g. 彼は耳ざとい *kare.wa mimi-zatoi* 'He has sharp ears'). Syntactic conditions to be met should thus be considered separately for each specific collocation.

3. Other criteria and the fuzzy distinction between compounds and collocations

When phonological or syntactic clues for compounding do not apply or are not decisive, one may take into consideration criteria that have more to do with the use or meaning of a given sequence. This seems particularly crucial for isolating languages in which the opposition between syntactic and lexical formations is unclear. Beyer (1992: 101ff.), on Tibetan, thus proposes three criteria "to determine whether an expression has been lexicalized in the language": (i) the frequency with which the expression occurs; (ii) the grammatical category of the expression; (iii) the semantic content of the expression.[43]

---

43 The first criterion should need a large corpus study that cannot be conducted here. The second criterion does not apply, since no change of grammatical category is expected in the case of SPC (see however the discussion in chap. 2 about changes involving a

A preliminary remark should be made about the terminology employed. It is preferable to speak of "lexicalized expressions" than "compounds". Indeed, high frequency and semantic idiomaticity are not properties of compounds only, but of collocations in general. In isolating languages, when the structure of a lexicalized expression takes on that of a free sequence, it is even more accurate to call it a collocation. Compounds, in the sense of "juxtaposition of two or more lexical stems" can be told apart from collocations in non-isolating languages because these languages do not usually allow simple juxtapositions of lexical stems to form phrases. Accordingly, as illustrated by Haspelmath, "German *Holzhaus* [wood-house] must be a compound because two juxtaposed nouns cannot form a noun phrase in German" (Haspelmath 2002: 154-155). In languages such as Thai, Chinese or Vietnamese, free sequences do however appear as mere juxtapositions of words, and 'mere juxtaposition' cannot be taken as a decisive criteria for compounding or lexicalization. Cf. the sequences "word-language-Thai" or "basis-rule-etymology" in the following Thai sentence:

(86) คำ|ภาษา|ไทย|ให้|เขียน|ตาม|หลัก|เกณฑ์|นิรุกติศาสตร์
kham phaasǎa thay hây khǐan taam làk keen nirúktisàat
word language Thai let write follow basis rule etymology
"Words in the Thai language should be written on the basis of principles of etymology." (Diller 1996: 466, in: Goddard 2005: 183)

The term 'collocation' can serve as a cover word for proper compounds as well as all kinds of lexicalized expressions. The need for a cover term becomes crucial from a contrastive perspective, even when contrasting two isolating languages. This view is substantiated by Post's (2007) contrastive comments about 'compounds' in Chinese and Thai. They cast doubts about the very existence of compounds in Thai:

"First, we show that while many functional morphemes in Mandarin

sequence 'N+active verb' becoming a descriptive verb).

> Chinese and Standard Thai derive from similar lexical sources, and emerge in the context of functionally and syntactically analogous constructions, the outcome is not in fact identical. Morphemes functioning grammatically in Chinese tend to attain a more advanced degree of structural readjustment than their counterparts in Thai. In this sense, they become more, or more deeply, grammaticalized. Next, we demonstrate that while patterns of lexical compounding in Thai and Chinese also resemble one another in being apparently widespread and structurally analogous, compounding is in fact deeper in Chinese than in Thai, as measured by such factors as frequency of occurrence, analyzability to speakers, and semantic shift. It is argued that these facts are plausibly correlated."

It is also more fruitful to describe Subject-Predicate sequences as collocations rather than compounds in Asian agglutinative languages. As will be seen in the following chapter, Subject-Predicate sequences that are sometimes termed 'compounds' in Korean, actually give little clue as to their syntactic cohesiveness. Even those Japanese sequences that undergo noun stripping (i.e. the loss of case particles) and sandhi processes, usually have corresponding full and *rendaku*-immune sequences *with the same meaning*. For instance, *hara-guroi* 'belly-black = black-hearted' alternates with *hara.ga kuroi* 'belly.S black'.

In other words, as in Chinese, many sequences may behave like words in some contexts, and like syntactic constructions in others. Nevertheless, they may retain properties of lexicalized sequences, so that they qualify for a collocation status.

This conclusion will be supported by tests of 'paradigmatic frozenness', through which the noun constituent is artificially put in the scope of contrastive constructions (see Chap. 3).

In this work, the semantic criterion of idiomaticity –called on for obvious reasons by many linguists, but not only, working on Chinese–, will often prove irrelevant. In several Asian languages, there are many instances of Subject-Predicate collocations that are perfectly transparent, not idiomatic. These are redundant SPC, illustrated for example by Korean *him.i seyta* 'energy/strength.S strong = strong'. They behave exactly contrary to the stricter version of the semantic criterion that Beyer (1996: 131) calls the 'semantic exocentricity' of the sequence, "where the meaning of the expression is not predictable from its components, and the head member of the collocation cannot be substituted for the whole without semantic change". They are nevertheless to be considered as collocations.

To sum up, the advantage of choosing the cover term 'collocation' over 'compound' is based on the following considerations:

(i) Clues for compounding may be scarce or inexistent in some languages, so that compounds can be equally well described as collocations;

(ii) Semantically and lexically identical sequences do not behave consistently with regard to their syntactic or phonological integrity. They may behave as frozen sequences in one context, and apparently as free sequences in another;

(iii) The contrastive point of view adopted here implies the comparison of sequences of structurally diverse languages that are equivalent from a broad semantic and functional perspective, but not necessarily equivalent from the perspective of their individual phonological and/or syntactic properties;

(iv) Some sequences that do not comply with any of the criteria mentioned in this chapter –including the semantic criterion of idiomaticity– will be under focus. These are still properly described as frozen sequences, or collocations.

Chap. 2

SPC in Standard Korean

This chapter focusses on SPC in the Korean standard language. Most of the data presented here are attested sentences picked up from various written or oral sources: blogs, newspapers, electronic letters, books, television, etc. As mentioned earlier, the recognition of compounding properties in Korean is not an easy task to undertake. One can actually doubt whether Subject Predicate *compounds* exist at all in Korean. The abbreviation "SPC" that will be used throughout this chapter should thus be read as "Subject-Predicate Collocation" rather than as "Subject-Predicate Compound", for reasons that should become clear in the course of this chapter. Along the same line as the preceding chapter, this chapter will inquire properties pertaining to different levels of analysis that could give hints for the integration of Subject-Predicate sequences. The data under investigation, that is, SPC or potential SPC, have been mainly gathered from (1) the literature on compounds or idioms, and (2) various monolingual or bilingual dictionaries.

A large majority of SPC may freely show up with or without the subject particle (*-i*/*-ka*), though some of them are usually recorded with it. In such a situation, it is noteworthy that a very small number of SPC has actually been fully lexicalized *with* the subject particle. For instance, 그지없다 *kuciepsta* 'limitless, endless', is a sequence incorporating the subject particle *-i*, derived from an older sequence *긏이 없다 *kuc.i epsta* 'end.Subj not_exist' (compare with modern Kor. 끝이 없다 *kkuth.i epsta* 'id.').

Leaving apart the intrusion of the subject marker (i.e. a grammatical morpheme), the sequence could qualify for the compound status: no lexical or grammatical word can intrude in the sequence, between the former subject and the predicate. *kuc* in the sense of 'end' can easily be related to modern *kkuth*, but it cannot occur in isolation. In addition, its phonetic shape cannot be derived from modern *kkuth* by any general rule, so that there is no way of considering the actual shape as a predictable allomorph required in composition.

The stative verb 가엽다 *kayep(s)ta* 'poor, pitiful, miserable' illustrates a similar case: it is an lexicalized SPC, derived from the Middle Kor. sequence *ka.i ep(s)ta*, meaning 'limit/end.S not_exist' (Cho H.B. 1992: 339ff.), the elements of which have merged. Here again, the (former) subject is a bound noun that does not occur in isolation in Modern Korean. The sequence cannot be broken, and furthermore, the incorporated subject particle *-i* attaches to a segment ending with a vowel, not a consonant as it would in Modern Korean, where *-ka* must be selected instead.

These examples show that Subject Predicate sequences can be lexicalized up to the point where they behave like simple words, but do not prove that there exist Subject-Predicate Compounds in Korean, since the nominal component would be hardly recognised as such in synchrony.

One apparently self-contradictory property of compounds is that they should have, as a whole, properties of words, while their internal constituents should also have word properties. The contradiction is only apparent because word properties are not to be checked within the lexicalized sequence. Components of compounds just have to occur as free constituents in other contexts. The subject noun in the examples above can actually be said to have at least one word property, more specifically one noun property, though only from a diachronic perspective, since it attaches a case marking particle. However, given that the (former) subject only occurs in a highly constrained sequence, and always with a same particle that cannot be dropped, it has no "distribution" in a syntactic sense, thus no belonging to a distributionally grounded class of nouns.

Lexicalized sequences of this kind cannot therefore be properly labeled "SPC", so that we shall concentrate on sequences in which the subject and the predicate have separate occurrences.

Before getting into the core question whether such sequences have compound properties or not, let us inquire more precisely what a subject looks like in Korean, and then try to set up a classification of the data.

1

General remarks

1. Subjects in Korean

At first view, Korean subjects, which we shall identify with sentence constituents marked by the particle *-i* (after consonants) or *–ka* (after vowels), look very much like subjects in most typical accusative languages: *-i*/*-ka* serves as a marker for (i) the sole argument of intransitive verbs, and (ii) the most agent-like argument of transitive verbs, while *-lul*/*-ul* marks the other argument (henceforth, the object):

-Sole argument.**ka** + Intransitive verb

(87) 까치가 울어서 [...]
*kkachi.**ka** wul.ese*
magpie.**S** cry.Con
"Because a magpie is crying..." (Yun Dong-ju, *An echo in the mountain*)

-Agent.**ka** + Patient.**ul** + Transitive verb

(88) 그가 아프가니스탄을 떠나는 것 [...]
*ku.**ka** aphukanisuthan.**ul** ttena.nun kes*
he.**S** Afghanistan.**Obj** leave.Adn fact
"... that he leaves Afghanistan." (*City*, 080118, p.10)

In addition, *-i*/*-ka* also marks the sole argument of any intransitive verb, including so-called unergative verbs such as *cry*, *sing*, *work*, etc., as well as unaccusative-type verbs, such as *sleep*, *come*, *die*, etc. Thus, as a whole, this system is seemingly close to that found in European languages such as English or French. A few facts are worth noting however. Among which:

- There do not exist dummy subjects such as Eng. *it* in *It's raining again*;
- There is a differential marking of the subject for the sake of subject's referent honorification (with a postposition *-kkeyse* probably related to the ablative/locative marking), or when the subject noun refers to a group or institution (with the ablative/locative postposition *-eyse*; see below (97);
- There is no agreement in person or number on the verb;
- Subject constituents may, just like other arguments or adjuncts, not be expressed at all.

This last property should have consequences on the definition of subjects in Korean, since Korean subjects, contrary to what we expect from core verbal arguments, thus behave much like adverbial adjuncts: they may be left out if their reference is clear from the context. In addition, subjects share the following property with temporal or locative adjuncts: in a (well-formed) sentence, composed of a single verb, it is always possible to add a subject constituent as well as a temporal or locative adjunct. This property is not shared by objects marked by *-lul/ul*. Contrast the acceptability of the following sentences with two intransitive descriptive verbs, *issta* 'exist, there is' and *manhta* 'numerous':

(89)	✓*issta*	exist	'(There) is (X)'
	→ ✓*cha.ka issta*	car.Nom exist	'(There) is a car'
	→ ✓*yeki.ey issta*	here.Loc exist	'(X) is here'
	→ ✓*yel.si.ey issta*	6.o'clock.Temp exist	'(There) is (X) at 6 o'clock'
	→ **kil.ul issta*	road.Acc exist	'??'

(90)	*manhta*	(be) many	'(There) are many (X)'
	→ ✓*cha.ka manhta*	car.S many	'(There) are many cars'
	→ ✓*yeki.ey manhta*	here.Loc many	'(There) are many (X) here'
	→ ✓*yel.si.ey manhta*	6.o'clock.Temp many	'(There) are many (X) at 6'
	→ **kil.ul manhta*	road.Obj many	'??'

The addressee role, marked by *-eykey* 'to', is much less restricted than the patient argument,[44] but may likewise be infelicitous with some specific verbs, like *pota* 'see':

(91)	✓*pwassta*	saw	'(X) saw (Y)'
	→ ✓*nay.ka pwassta*	I.S saw	'I saw (Y)'
	→ ✓*yeki.ey pwassta*	here.Loc saw	'(X) saw (Y) here'
	→ ✓*yel.si.ey pwassta*	6.o'clock.Temp saw	'(X) saw (Y) at 6 o'clock'
	→ **T.eykey pwassta*	T.Dat saw	'??'

If the property of "ubiquitous felicity" thus allows to tell apart subjects from other core arguments, distinguishing subjects from adjuncts is not such an easy task. It is often argued that arguments, hence including subjects, should have specific semantic features that are required by the main predicate. Such required features are known as "selectional restrictions" or "selectional preferences". For instance, in the following example, the subject of the verb *wusta* 'laugh' must refer to an animate being for the sentence to be felicitous (Nam K.S. 2005: 77):

(92) *소나무가 웃는다.
sonamwu.ka wus.nun.ta
pine_tree.S laugh.Pres.TS
"*The pine tree laughs."

---

44 It may indeed susbtitute to the subject marker in experiencer or possessive clauses.

According to the same author – but this bias is pervasive in the literature[45] –, the same kind of restriction does not apply to adverbial adjuncts, which are said not to be "dependent on specific predicates" (Nam K.S. 2005: 152).

Yet locative adjuncts are also referentially constrained. In the following two examples from the same author, the substitution of the original locative adjuncts for respectively an abstract (*yaksok* 'promise') and an animate entity (*chinkwu* 'friend') gives ungrammatical sentences:

(93) 아이들이 마당/*약속에서 뛰논다.
ai.tul.i matang.eyse ttwino.n.ta
chil.Plur.S yard.Loc play.Pres.TS
"Children are playing in the yard."
vs.
**ai.tul.i yaksok.eyse ttwino.n.ta*
"Children are playing in the promise ."

(94) 산/*친구에 진달래가 피었다.
san.ey cintallay.ka phi.ess.ta
mountain.Loc azalea.S bloom.Past.TS
"Azaleas bloomed in the mountain."
vs.
**chinkwu.ey cintallay.ka phi.ess.ta*
friend.Loc azalea.Nom bloom.Past.TS
"Azaleas bloomed in the friend."

It could be argued that locative arguments exclude, by definition, animate or abstract entities. This reasoning is however not only circular, it is also false, given that animate or abstract entities may also be licensed with a locative particle,[46] as in:

45 Often implicitly though, since selectional restrictions are usually illustrated with arguments only. E.g., "We refer to the restrictions imposed by the predicates of the sentences above *on their arguments as selectional restrictions*." (Aarts 2001: 98)

46 Even if one excludes examples of metaphorical uses (e.g. *ppacita* 'fall' in *sarang.ey ppacita* 'fall in love' or *sayngkak.ey ppacita* 'be absorbed in a thought / be sold on an idea'). Example (95) may be rejected as clumsy by some native speakers (I. Choi-Jonin,

(95) 어느 베트남 엄마에서 태어난 자녀의 눈물 (http://v.daum.net/link/21923206)
enu peythunam emma.eyse thayena.n canye.uy nwunmul
some Vietnam mum.Source be_born.Adn:Past children.Gen tears
"Tears of children born from a Vietnamese mother."

(96) 그 생각에 문제가 있기 때문이다.
ku sayngkak.ey muncey.ka iss.ki_ttaymun.i.ta
this idea.Loc problem.S exist.because.Cop.TS
"Because there's a problem in this idea."

There are thus selectional restrictions on arguments as well as on adjuncts, so that this criterion does not tell apart subjects from locative adjuncts. In addition, Korean subjects can be stacked, as adjuncts do as well.

Yet some properties are specific to subjects, such as the mandatory *-si-* suffixing on the verb for subject honorification, or the optional change of case marking (from subject to object or dative) in causative constructions, but one can wonder whether such properties are not bound to the fact that subjects, being typically animate and dotted with volition, may be the target of respect or causation, while locative adjuncts are not. The main difference between subjects and locative adjuncts would therefore be semantically rather than syntactically grounded. The reader is reminded here that logical subjects referring to inanimate referents, such as institutions, are usually precisely marked with the locative/ablative postposition *-eyse*:

(97) 영국 식품표준국에서는 이미 임신 여성에 대해 참치를 피하라고 권고하고 있다.
yengkwuk sikphum.phyocwun.kwuk.eyse.nun imi imsin yeseng.ey_tayhay chamchi.lul phiha.lako kwenkoha.ko_iss.ta

pers. comm.), but such examples are not rare.

UK food.standard.office.**Abl**.Top already pregnant woman. regarding tuna.Obj avoid.Quot:Imp recommend.Prog.TS
"The Food Standards Agency of the United Kingdom is already recommending that pregnant women avoid eating tuna". (Kang Chang-soo, editorial, *Joongang Ilbo*, 080201)

Therefore, subjects in Korean could be defined as sentence constituents (1) that can always appear in a sentence, and (2) that refer to the most agent-like argument of the main predicate, when the main predicate is unmarked for voice (e.g. passive) or diathesis (e.g. causative). Since this second criteria may prove delicate in specific cases, it is possible to state a more general property in paradigmatic terms: a subject, which ever its actual reference may be, belongs to a paradigm in which it is always possible to find constituents commuting with one of the following two interrogative proforms: *nwukwu* 'who' and *mues* 'what'.

The profiling of Korean subjects does not end here, since there is another property that proves very important for our concern: As was seen in Chapter 1, in some specific but numerous constructions, the subject particle can be used to mark the most agent-like argument *and* the most patient-like argument of a transitive verb. That is to say, some predicates do not display a proper "syntactic alignment"; instead, two core arguments of a single predicate get the same marking as the sole argument of an intransitive verb. As a typical case for such constructions, let us have a look at sentences referring to psychological events involving a stimulus experienced by an animate being.[47] These sentences will be referred to as "**stimulus-experiencer**" sentences, e.g.:

-Experiencer.*ka* + Stimulus.*ka* + Transitive verb

(98)	내**가**	이타리아**가**	자주	그리워요.
	*nay.**ka***	*ithalia.**ka***	*cacwu*	*kuliwe.yo*
	I.S	Italy.**S**	often	miss.TS

"I often miss Italy."

47 There are also one-place emotive predicates such as 외롭다 *oylopta* 'lonesome'.

Such a situation explains why Korean psychological state verbs are usually rendered in bilingual dictionaries both as experiencer-oriented adjectives and as stimulus-oriented adjectives. One can, for instance, find the following equivalents to 기쁘다 *kipputa*: "delighted" or "delightful", "pleasant" or "pleased", etc. This double orientation of Korean psychological verbs is often a source of mistakes for Korean speakers of European languages, who may have trouble in deciding which adjective fits with an experiencer or stimulus subject. The following are typical illustrations of what could be called the 'Pointing Sister Construction', since it is best illustrated with the sentence 'I'm so exciting' in (99)[48]:

(99) *I'm coming back to Korea this June!! I'm so exciting:)*
(Kim J.H., 25.01.08)

(100) *you have a many friend~ / I'm surprising* ^^*
(Lee D.H, 15.02.08)

(101) *its really happy for me to get your news.* (SHH, 21.06.99)

In Korean stimulus-experiencer sentences, each subject may be left out without damage to the grammaticality of the sentence. If only one subject is expressed, ambiguity can be expected to arise as to whether the subject is the experiencer or the stimulus. This does not happen, because verbs referring to psychological processes have two forms: the one given above is, roughly speaking, mostly restricted to the ego's state in assertive sentences, while the other, using the same root expanded by means of the auxiliary verb *hata* 'do', is used for describing somebody else's feelings, e.g.:

(102) 태희가 자주 그리워요.
thayhuy.ka cacwu kuliwe.yo
Taehee.S often miss.TS
"(I) often miss Taehee." vs. *"Taehee often miss (X)"

48 Instead of 'I'm so excited', which was the title of a song sung by the once famous band *The Pointer Sisters*.

(103) 태희가 자주 그리워해요.
thayhuy.ka cacwu kuliwe.hay.yo
Taehee.S often miss.do.TS
*"(I) often miss Taehee." vs. "Taehee often miss (X)"

The second construction follows the accusative alignment, with the experiencer marked as a subject, and the stimulus marked as an object.

Another common type of sentence with two subjects involves the existential-possessive construction, expressed by means of the verbs 있다 *issta* "be, exist" or 없다 *epsta* "not_exist". E.g.:

(104) 정말 내가 돈이 있어도 안사겠다는 생각이 든다. (pann.nate.com/b1599734)
cengmal nay.ka ton.i iss.eto an.sa.keyss.ta.nun sayngkak.i tu.n.ta
really I.S money.S exist.although Neg.buy.Fut.Quot.Adn thought.S enter.Pres.TS
"Really, even though I have money, I think I won't buy (it)."

(105) 그리구 저희 어머니 아버지가 차가 없어요. (www.mypet.or.kr/v2.0/board/view.asp?)
kulikwu cehuy emeni apeci.ka cha.ka epse.yo
and we mother father.S car.S not_exist.Pol
"And my ("our") parents don't have a car."

Similar constructions frequently involve a body-part and a verb of specific meaning, in which case it is used for describing somebody's physical characteristics:

(106) 명식은 손이 크다.
myengsik.un son.i khuta
Myeongsik.Top hand.S big
"(Lit. As for Myeongsik hands are big) Myeongsik has big hands."[49]

But there is a broad range of possible relationships between the first subject (possessor) and the second subject (possessed), and more than two subjects may be involved, as shown in the following examples from Kuno (2004: 102) or Song J.J. (2005: 111):[50]

(107) 아버님이 옷이 소매가 찢어지셨다.
apenim.i os.i somay.ka cciceci.sy.ess.ta
father.S clothes.S sleeve.S torn.Hon.Past.TS
"As for father, the sleeves of his clothes are torn."

(108) 기호가 자동차가 문이 손잡이가 깨끗하다
kiho.ka catongcha.ka mun.i soncapi.ka kkaykkusha.ta
Keeho.S car.S door.S handle.S clean.ST
"The handle on the door of Keeho's car is clean."

Stimulus-experiencer as well as possessive-existential constructions are fully productive in the sense that they provide subject slots that can be fulfilled by a wide variety of noun phrases. In other terms, as long as the referents of the subject nouns meet the selection restrictions provided by the predicate, the argument slots allow paradigmatic variation. The same remark can be made about the predicate slot. Predicates in stimulus-experiencer patterns include descriptive verbs such as *mipta* 'hateful (hate)', *cohta* 'likeable (like)', *musepta* ' dreadful (fear)', etc., while the verb *issta* 'exist' in possessive-existential sentences can, in most cases, be substituted for other verbs of existence, as *epsta* 'not exist', *manhta* 'be many', *sayngkita* 'arise, come into being', etc. Examples (with an animate and an inanimate possessee):

49 In a metaphorical sense, also 'be generous'.
50 As mentioned by the author, "more than three or four nominative-marked noun phrases in a single, simple sentence may sound contrived or unnatural." (Song J.J., 2005: 111)

(109)	X에게/가	애인이 / 돈이	없다 *epsta* 'not exist'
	X.*eykey/ka*	*ayin.i / ton.i*	많다 *manhta* 'be many'
	X.Dest/S	lover.S / money.S	생겼다 *sayngky.ess.ta* 'arose'

'X {doesn't have, have many, got} a (boy/girl)friend(s) / money.'[51]

Paradigmatic variation will be more remarkable if one takes into account closely related patterns that also involve a meronymic relationship between the two subjects, as in the above examples (e.g. 106).

Since potential SPC in Korean often share the same two-or-more-subjects argument frame with these constructions, it will be useful to keep them in mind as a point of comparison when investigating SPC candidates. It is however expected that the relationship between the subject and the predicate of the latter should prove tighter. Let us now consider some hints as to what could constitute a good SPC candidate in Korean.

2. Word-like availability of Subject-Predicate sequences

As pointed out in the introduction, compounds as well as collocations, differently from regular phrases or sentences, should have some sort of word-like availability in the speaker's competence: in other words, they are not thought of as being built on-line; rather they belong to the speaker's mental lexicon. It shall not be attempted to know what is going on inside the Korean speaker's mind, but here are some hints that help in gathering the data, though none of them is decisive:

Firstly, more or less convincing but helpful for eliciting data, several subject-predicate sequences are usually written as one word, in a context

51 Numerous instances can be found online, e.g.: 할아버지가 애인이 생겼어요 *halapeci.ka ayin.i sayngky.ess.e.yo* 'Grandpa has (got) a girl friend' (http://pann.nate.com/talk/201733795).

where in (Modern) Korean, contrary to languages such as Japanese, Chinese or Thai, makes use of blank spaces between phrases. Spelling is certainly a matter of convention and is subject to normalization, but it is clearly related to the linguistic consciousness of the literate part of a given population. Note that introduction of blank spaces is mandatory when the subject particle is attached to the subject component. Contrast for instance the following alternatives (A '*' indicates that the sequence is not acceptable according to standard spelling conventions):

(110)	재미있다 *caymi-issta* interest-exist	vs.	*재미 있다 *caymi issta* interest-exist
(111)	*재미가있다 *caymi.ka-issta* interest-SUB-exist	vs.	재미가 있다 *caymi.ka issta* interest-SUB-exist

Secondly, contrary to what has been said about the optionality of the subject in Korean, the subject constituent in SPC is usually very difficult to drop out.[52]

Thirdly, many SP sequences are singled out as main entries in Korean monolingual and bilingual dictionaries.

Fourthly, if Korean speakers are asked to provide words denoting "fatigue, tiredness" or "difficulty", it is quite likely that they will list *him-tulta* 'energy-enter' together with simple words such as 버겁다 *pekepta* 'be hard (beyond one's capacity)' or 어렵다 *elyepta* 'difficult, hard'. In contrast, it is impossible to find a simple word that could be listed alongside with the Korean equivalent sequences to "car exist" or "miss Italy", even though these sequences have the same grammatical structure as Subject-Predicate collocations.

Fifthly, and this property is related to the latter, many subject-predicate sequences behave –functionally speaking– as independent lexical items: they have functional expansions or compatibilities of

52 The first two properties are actually shared by support verb constructions.

their own that cannot be derived from the functional properties of their components. In that sense, they can again be said to commute with simple words. This should imply that subjects in SPC are not external arguments of the predicate but belong to the verb phrase. These properties will be inquired in §2.3(p. 154).

Looking for data matching one or more of the preceding properties allows to easily gather a large corpus of more than 500 items, among which one can, more or less arbitrarily, recognize complex words, compounds, collocations, or support verb constructions.

3. Towards a classification of Korean SPC

What is proposed here is a classification of SPC according to syntactic criteria, in terms of compatibility with other elements in the sentence or in terms of "transformational" properties. This classification will help in checking the functional particulars of SPC compared to those of their internal constituents.

As stated above, SPC enter valency frames usually allowing two constituents overtly marked as subjects, including that of the SPC. In the following schematization, Y stands for the subject component of the SPC, X for another constituent possibly marked with the subject particle (postposition *-i*/*-ka* represented by S):

(112) X.(S) [Y.(S) Predicate]$_{\text{SPC}}$

The first line of separation will be drawn between SPC in which the subject status of either X or Y is questionable.

(i) Type A: Collocations describing natural phenomena

The first class isolates events referring to natural phenomena such as 'to rain', 'to snow', '(for the day) to break', etc., which are expressed in Korean, as in many other languages, as intransitive sentences with a referential subject, e.g. Kor. 'rain-come', Ch./Jap. 'snow-fall', etc. Such sequences display a high degree of collocation, both in terms of frequency and of paradigmatic restriction. Paradigmatic alternation between co-hyponyms may however be allowed. In Kor. *pi.ka ota* 'rain.S come', the verb *ota* can be replaced by *naylita* 'go/come down'[53] (same meaning), or by its antonyms *kata* 'go' or *cinakata* 'pass', and even be coordinated:

(113) 다행히 비가 오고 지나가서 날씨가 선선해진거같은데...[54]
tahaynghito pi.ka o.ko cinaka.se nalssi.ka sensenhayci.n ke_kath.untay
fortunately rain.S come.Con pass.Cause weather.S cool_down.Adn:Past.seem.Con
"Fortunately, now that (lit.) the rain came and passed off, it seems that the weather cooled down."

A hint of their word-like availability will be however pointed out in the following chapter. One can also observe that some of these sequences can serve as a base for secondary derivations, as in Kor. *hay-tot-i* 'sunrise', which are derived nominals stemming respectively from *hay.(ka) totta* 'sun.(S) rise' (cf. Jap. *ame-fur-i* from *ame.(ga) furu* 'rain.(S) fall').

Meteorological subject-predicate sentences can be set apart from other sequences because of their poor compliance to the 'X.(S) [Y.(S) Predicate]' pattern. They may indeed follow another constituent marked with the subject particle *-ka*, as in:

(114) 여기가 비가 왔다.
yeki.ka *pi.ka wa.ss.ta*
here.S rain.S come.Past.TS
"(It is) here (that) it rained."

This constituent is necessarily interpreted as the location of the event, and behaves differently from regular subjects. First, in accordance with its locative interpretation, it cannot commute with the proform *mues* 'what' or *nwukwu* 'who', but with the locative proform *eti* 'where'. Second, the subject particle itself can be substituted for a locative particle

53 But *wupak* 'hail' only accepts *ota* 'come', not *naylita*. Cf. also *nal.i sayta/tulta* 'day.S break_through/enter = dawn'.

54 http://cafe430.daum.net/_c21_/bbs_search_read

(*-(ey)se*), which is not normally licensed with subjects:[55]

(115) 여기서 비가 왔다.
yeki.se *pi.ka wa.ss.ta*
here.Loc rain.S come.PAST.TS
"It rained here."

Examples of this type (Type A) include:

비가 오다	*pi.ka ota*	rain + come	'rain'
해가 돋다	*hay.ka totta*	sun + come up	'(for the sun to) rise'
날이 들다	*nal.i tulta*	day + enter	'(for the day to) break'

(ii) Type B: Complex words

For the second class, the problem arises from the status of Y, not X, as a subject. There are sequences such as *ko-toyta* (fatigue-become) 'exhausting' in which we know from the verb *toyta* that the preceding constituent should be a subject, but it is impossible to insert a subject particle –or any other segment– between the putative subject constituent and the verb (**ko.ka toyta*), so that such highly fusioned sequences are again excluded from the [X'.(S) X.(S) Predicate] frame. To this group can be added those sequences already evoked in the introduction of this chapter in which the case marker has been phonologically integrated, to the point that the sequence is not segmentable anymore in synchrony (cf. *kuciepsta* 'limitless' and *kayepsta* 'miserable'). To put it differently, the SP segment behaves like a single word under all perspectives, but its subject constituent does not display the morphological properties of a regular subject. In Korean, as already mentioned, such sequences cannot be properly labeled as compounds, because the first constituent has no autonomy in any other context.

Examples of Type B either have a Sino-Korean pseudo-noun or an

55 Except in specific conditions, as stated above, with subjects referring to institutions, groups, etc.

inherited Korean noun as their Y constituent:

축나다	*chwuk-nata*	lack + arise	'decrease, decline'
주되다	*cwu-toyta*	chief, head + become	'main, major'[56]
가엽다	*kayepta*	limit.(†S) + not_exist	'pathetic, pitiful'
그지없다	*kuciepsta*	end.(†S) + not_exist	'limitless, endless'

(iii) Type C and Type D: non gradable and gradable SPC

Other SPC enter a frame that can be properly labeled as a 'double subject construction', even though the two subjects X and Y have different properties, and none can be regarded as gathering all subject properties by itself.

Two subcategories C and D will be further distinguished depending on how X' can be associated with a complement of the comparative.

In Korean, the comparative is built as follows: the comparative element is marked with the suffix *pota* 'than/in comparison with'. As the more accurate translation, 'in comparison with', may suggest, the superiority sense is a default interpretation of the predicate if there is no additional adverb (like *te* 'more' or *tel* 'less'), as in the following example:

(116) 여자보다 예쁜 남자
yeca.pota yeyppu.n namca
woman.Stand pretty.Adn man
"A man pretty in comparison with a woman = A man prettier than a woman"

Here, *te* 'more' can also be optionally added before the verb, while if the inferiority sense is intended, *tel* 'less' is obligatory. The ability of accepting a complement of the comparative without an additional adverb can be taken as a syntactic property discriminating adjective-like verbs from other verbs. Compare for example the last sentence with a

56 This word is mainly used as an adnominal predicate, e.g. *cwutoy.n wen'in* 'main.Adn reason = the main reason'.

similar sequence involving *ilhata* 'work':

(117) *남보다 일하는 사람
nam.pota ilha.nun salam
other.Stand work.Adn person
"A person that works in comparison with others"

The sequence is infelicitous unless one inserts either the adverb *te* 'more' (or *tel*), another adverb, or both:

(118) *nam.pota* ***te*** */* ***ppalli*** *ilha.nun salam*
other.Stand more / quickly work.Adn person
"A person that works more / more quickly than others"

A contrast similar to the opposition *yepputa* 'pretty' and *ilhata* 'work' can be found in SPC as well. The feature to be checked can be stated as follows:

[± X"-*pota* X.(S) Y.(S) Pred]

The following examples will illustrate whether the subject X in a [X.(S) Y.(S) Pred] sentence can be contrasted with another constituent serving as an element of comparison.

In (119), the sequence *kwi.ka mek.(ta)* 'ear.S eat = get deaf' qualifying the subject 'guys around me', in comparison with 'the average people' would be unnatural unless the adverb *te* 'more' is inserted:

(119) 내 주위에 있는 녀석들이 평범한 사람들보다 더 귀가 먹었거나 [...]
*nay cwuwi.ey iss.nun nyesek.tul.i phyengpemha.n salam.tul.***pota te** *kwi.ka mek.ess.kena*
my surrounding.Loc be.Adn fellows.Plur.S average.Adn people.Plur.pota **more** ear.S eat.Past.or
"[...] or (that) the guys around me got deafer than the average people."

→ ?*salam.tul.**pota** kwi.ka mek.ess.e* ~ ✓✓*salam.tul.**pota te** kwi.ka mek.ess.e*

In contrast to this situation, the SPC *caymi.issta* 'interest.exist = be interesting, funny' can freely appear with or without *te*:

(120) 확실히 공포영화보다 재미있더라고요.[57]
hwaksilhi kongpho.yenghwa.pota caymi.iss.te.lakwu.yo
surely horror.movie.Stand interest.exist.Ret.Quot.TS
"(I tell you,) it was definitely funnier than a horror movie."
→ ✓*kongpho.yenghwa.**pota** caymi.iss.e* ~ ✓*kongpho.yenghwa.**pota te** caymi.iss.e*

Examples of the first group (hence, Type C) typically include punctual or inchoative predicates:

생각이 나다	*sayngkak.i nata*	thought + arise	'come to mind, remember'
말이 나다	*mal.i nata*	word + arise	'be brought into conversation'
병이 들다	*pyeng.i tulta*	sickness + enter	'get/fall ill'
싹이 돋다	*ssak.i totta*	bud + come up/rise	'put forth new shoots'
귀가 먹다	*kwi.ka mekta*	ear + eat	'get deaf'

Examples of Type D are usually composed of a stative predicate that would be translated as an adjective in English, but this is not a necessary condition. The last example, *mas-nata* 'taste-arise = be tasty', is formed out of an inchoative verb.

57 (http://danmee.chosun.com/site/data/html_dir/2009/11/03/2009110303006.html)

머리가 좋다	*meli.ka cohta*	head + good	'quick-witted'
나이가 젊다	*nai.ka celmta*	age + young	'young'
손이 크다	*son.i khuta*	hand + big	'generous'
힘이 세다	*him.i seyta*	strength + strong	'strong'
값이 싸다	*kaps.i ssata*	price + cheap	'cheap'
귀가 밝다	*kwi.ka palkta*	ear + clear	'sharp-eared'
맛이 나다	*mas.i nata*	taste + arise	'be tasty'

Now, putting all criteria together enables us to ventilate the data in four categories as follows:

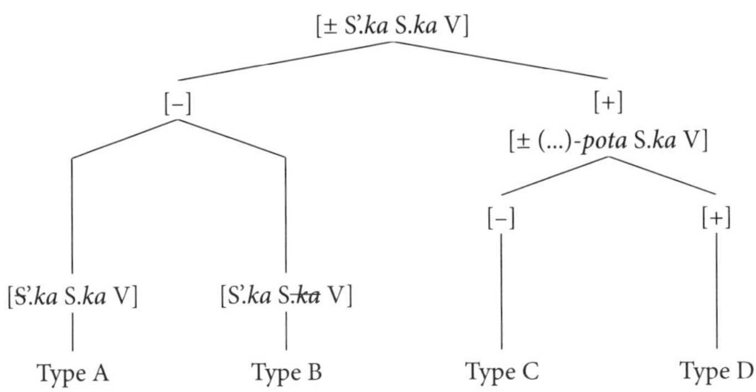

Such a classification, according to (i) whether the SPC can be described as a 'double subject construction', and (ii), whether the whole sequence has adjective-like properties in the sense that it does not need additional segment to be gradable, could be applied to other languages as well, and thus allow cross-linguistic comparisons. Note that the gradability test could be applied to sequences of Types A and B as well, but this would be irrelevant, since their primary characteristics naturally set them apart.

The next section, focusing on the properties of Korean SPC, will show that most compound properties that can be tested do not give positive results for the majority of sequences. A few syntactic hints towards their wordhood will however be proposed, for which the classification above into types C and D will prove helpful.

2

An overview of integration properties

For the properties reviewed in the following pages, two things are worth noticing. Firstly, several subject predicate sequences have conflicting or contradictory properties in terms of integration. In other words, they might behave as frozen sequences from a certain perspective but as free sequences from another. Secondly, as a whole, and because many tests have a low applicability, the results of the investigation give a rather impressionistic picture.

Let us first discuss properties of SPC that do not qualify them as compounds.

1. Phonological changes

1) Phonologically conditioned changes

Korean is a language where numerous phonotactic constraints and changes affect the basic phonological form of words or morphemes. For instance, the phonetic realization of a given string allows only one consonant in syllable final position (coda) to be realized. Other examples are obligatory resyllabification when a consonant in a coda is followed by a vowel, or total assimilation of one consonant in *n-l* or *l-n* sequences, thus becoming *l-l* or, more rarely, *n-n*.

Such phenomena are seen as automatic alternations, at least as far as the domain of word (and compound) formation, is concerned. If idiosyncratic behaviours can be observed with lexical or grammatical suffixes, these are well-known and described. It is however not yet clear to what extent they apply to formations above the word level. In other words, would such rules apply to any kind of syntactic formation?

The answer to this question has to be negative, as syntactic formations may involve optional or necessary pauses, or hesitations, that would forbid in most cases the application of the rules described below. It is however altogether true that several studies suggest that most if not all phonological processes may also apply to syntactic formations that can be considered as free sequences. It would therefore be adventurous to conclude from the fact that SPC undergo phonological processes observed for words that they are necessary words as well.

In the following are listed some of the major sound alternations in Korean (from Sohn H.M. 1999: 164-176; see also Kim M.R. 2002: 733), with illustrations taken among SP collocations.

(1) Cluster reduction: CC / ____ {C, #, +} →	C
값나가다 *kaps-nakata* 'price-go out = be expensive'	['ka**m**.na.ka.ta][58]
(2) Coda neutralization:	
{t, th, s, ss, c, ch, h} {p, (ph), pp} / ____ {C, #, +} → {k, kh, kk}	[t] [p] [k]
낯없다 *nach-epsta* 'face-not_exist = ashamed' 덧없다 *tes-epsta* 'short_time-not_exist = short-lived'	[na.'**t**ep.tta] [te.'**t**ep.tta]
(3) Resyllabification: V(C)C.(G/h)V	→ V(C).C(G/h)V
독오르다 *tok-oluta* 'poison-rise = become poisonous'	[to.'**k**o.lu.ta]
(4) Lateralization: {l, n} / l ____ →	[l]
길나다 *kil-nata* 'road-arise = get used to' 골나다 *kol-nata* 'anger-arise = be in anger'	['kil.**l**a.ta] ['kol.**l**a.ta]

58 The cluster [ps] is first simplified to [p] (see consonant cluster simplification), then assimilated to [m].

(5) Nasal assimilation: C (other than l) / ____ C[+nasal]	→ homorganic nasal
바닥나다 *patak-nata* 'floor-arise = get used up'	[pa.'ta**ng**.na.ta]
끝나다 *kkuth-nata* 'end-arise = end'	['kku**n**.na.ta]
빛나다 *pich-nata* 'light-arise = shine'	['pi**n**.na.ta]
목마르다 *mok-maluta* 'throat-dry = be thirsty'	['mo**ng**.ma.lu.ta]
뜻맞다 *ttus-macta* 'meaning/wish-fit = be like-minded, be to one's taste'	['ttu**n**-mat.tta]

(6) Tensification: C[+lax] / {p, t, k} ____ →	C[+tensed]
색다르다 *sayk-taluta* 'color-different = strange'	['sayk.**tt**a.lu.ta]
맛들다 *mas-tulta* 'taste-enter = become tasty'	['mat.**tt**ul.ta]
값지다 *kaps-cita* 'price-become = valuable, expensive'	[kap.**cc**i.ta]
낯설다 *nach-selta* 'face-unripe = unfamiliar'	[na(s).'**ss**el.ta]

The first two processes, final cluster reduction and coda neutralization, occur before a pause (#) or at compound boundaries (+). Let us take the words 닭 /talk/ 'chicken' and 짚 /ciph/ 'straw'. The segments /lk/ and /ph/ posited in the phonological transcriptions are actually never observed *as syllable codas* in the actual output of the respective sequences. The sequence /lk/ in the first word can be observed before a vowel initial suffix, such as the subject suffix *-i*, *talk.i*, with the second consonant being carried over to the onset of the following syllable ([tal.ki]). /lk/ is however reduced to [k] before a pause as well as in compounds, e.g. 닭고기 *talk.koki* [tak.kko.ki] 'chicken meat'.

The same happens to consonants that are neutralized to their corresponding plain consonants. For instance, the aspirated consonant /ph/ is realized before the subject suffix *-i* (*ciph.i* [ci.phi]), but is neutralized to [p] if the word *ciph* appears in isolation or as the first element of a compound, e.g.: *ciph.sin* [cip.ssin] 'straw shoes'.[59]

Noteworthy is the fact that if the second element of a compound has an initial vowel, the coda of the first element will be equally reduced and/or neutralized, even though the final consonant could be carried over to the next syllable as is the case with vocalic grammatical suffixes

59 The tensification of the following onset consonant in [tak.*kk*o.ki] and [cip.*ss*in] results from the automatic tensification rule after [p] and [k].

(Sohn H.M. 1999: 166):

	Meaning	Phonological form	Expected	Realized
값어치	'price-worth = value'	/kaps-echi/	*[kap.se.chi]	[ka.pe.chi]
밭알	'field-seed = red-bean grains'	/path-al/	*[pa.thal]	[pa.tal]

The neutralized final consonant can further undergo various other phonological processes, such as resyllabification, lateralization, nasal assimilation, sonorization,[60] etc., that are also observed at the word-internal level. A nice example of the successive application of such rules would be the sequence 짚여물 *ciph.yemul* 'straw fodder', the output of which can be seen as the result of three rules: (1) final consonant neutralization: *[ci**p**.yemul]; (2) *n*-insertion before the semi-vowel [y] in non-initial position: *[cip.**n**yemul]; (3) subsequent nasal assimilation of [p]: [ci**m**.nyemul].

As mentioned above, SPC regularly undergo these phonetic changes. This does however not mean that they are compounds, or even any kind of frozen collocation. The same phonetic changes will also occur in linked speech within free syntactic constructions.

Resyllabification or nasalization are for instance observed in SPC (see above *tok-oluta* 'poison-rise' [to.**ko**.lu.ta] and *mok-maluta* 'throat-dry' [mo**ng**.ma.lu.ta], but also in the following sequences formed out of the modal adverb *kkok* 'without fail' and any verb that would be appropriate[61]:

(121) 꼭 오세요 [꼬고세요]
kkok o.sey.yo [kko.**ko**.sey.yo]
without_fail come.Hon.TS
"Please (make sure that you) come by."

60 Sonorization is not listed above and normally not reflected in our transcription, but it regularly occurs between vowels, e.g. [pa.tal] should be read as [pa.dal].

61 See also in sequences of family and given names, e.g.: 박명희 *pak.myeng.hi* → [pa**ng**.myeng.i] 'Pak Myung-hee' (a former president's name).

(122) 꼭 누르세요.
kkok nwulu.sey.yo [kko**ng** nwu.lu.sey.yo]
without_fail press.Hon.TS
"Make sure that you push (the button)."

The next example shows that nasalization can even occur between constituents that are both "heavy", whether in terms of phonological or syntactic "load": an adverbial adjunct and an object (pro)noun. As it is drawn from a song, the nasal realization of the coda /k/ can be easily confirmed:

(123) 오천년속 널 기다린 바다속으로 [...] (*Crying Nut*, 물밑의 속삭임)
o.chen.nyen.sok ne.l kitali.n pata.sok.ulo [...] [so**ng** # **n**el]
5.000.year.inside you.Obj wait.Adn:Past sea.inside.Dir
"[...] to the sea (where X / which) has been waiting for you for 5000 years."

Kang E.G. (2002: 138), on the other hand, provides examples of coda neutralization and subsequent sonorization in free argument-verb or argument-argument sequences:

(124) 짚 이고
ciph i.ko [ci**b**igo]
straw carry.and
"carrying straw on the head"

(125) 꽃 어디 있어?
koch eti i.ss.e [ko**d**ediisse]
flower where be.FS
"Where is the flower?"

Ko S.Y. (2002: 50), discussing the domain of application of the change /n/ → /l/ next to the consonant /l/, suggests local restrictions when the order is /ln/ rather than /ln/ but clearly indicates that the lateralization rule is not limited to the formation of simple or compound words.[62] In the following excerpt from a famous Kim Gwang-Seok's song, the change /n/ → /l/ in the initial of the verb, triggered by the object particle *-ul*, can clearly be heard (see also (127)):

(126) 잉어만이 한숨을 내쉰다.
ing'e.man.i hanswum.ul nayswi.n.ta [hanswum.ul **l**ayswinta]
carp.only.S breath.Obj breathe_out.Pres.FS
"Only the carp lets out a sigh."

(127) 아들을 낳다
atul.ul nah.ta [atu.lul **l**a.tha]
son.Obj give_birth
"give birth to a son"

The domain of tensification is probably more suggestive of the integration of some syntactic phrases. Tensification refers to the fact that the initial plain consonant of a syllable is pronounced tense (if it has a tense counterpart) after an obstruent (i.e. [p, t, c, k, etc.], but not after [m, n, l]). This phonological process is obligatory within words, e.g. in 낙성대 *naksengtay* [nakssengtay] (place name). It is also observed in the standard pronunciation of collocational sequences, and precisely in argument- or adjunct predicate sequences such as:

(128) 맛보다 *mas-pota* [ma**t**-**pp**ota] 'taste-see = taste (try)';
시집가다 *sicip-kata* [sici**p**-**kk**ata] 'husband's home-go = get married (for women)';
속상하다 *sok-sanghata* [so**k**-**ss**anghata] 'inside-get sour = feel bad';
색다르다 *sayk-taluta* [say**k**-**tt**aluta] 'colour-different = original, out of the way'.

The main condition is that no pause is realized between the noun

62 "유음화는 단일어든 복합어든 상관없이 낱말의 내부에서, 또 낱말 경계가 개입하는 통사적 구성 등에서 음운론적 환경만 맞으면 언제든지 나타나는 동화 현상이다."

phrase and the verb.

In free combinations of noun-phrases and verbs, on the contrary, the initial consonant of the verb is not supposed to undergo tensification in the proper context, so that the final [p] of *cangkap* 'glove' would normally not trigger a change [p] to [pp] in *pakkuta* 'change':

(129) 장갑 바꿨어.
cangkap pakkw.ess.e ?* [cangka**p** **pp**akkwesse]
glove change.Past.FS
"(I) changed (my) gloves."

As suggested by Kim Hyun (pers. comm.), tensification could however occur in this example in rapid speech if the sentence is inserted in a larger unit where it would form an intonational unit. Tensification in this case would not be accompanied by a higher pitch on the following vowel as it would typically with inherently tense consonants in word-initial contexts.[63]

Such incomplete tensification is more likely to occur in sequences that would be more common in daily speech -but still not collocations-, such as those formed with X 주세요 *cwuseyyo* '(please) give (me) X', e.g.:

(130) (담배) 한 갑 주세요
(tampay) han kap cwu.sey.yo [ka**p** cwuseyyo] / ([ka**p** **c**cwuseyyo])
(cigarette) one NumCl give.Hon.FS
"One pack (of cigarettes), please."

Whereas it would be almost(?) obligatory in the ritual blessing for the Korean New Year's day: 복 받으세요 *pok patuseyyo* [po**k** **pp**atuseyyo] '(lit.) Receive happiness'.

It is doubtful whether many people would agree to consider such ritual formulae as compounds, hence as words rather than as

63 This discussion of tensification greatly benefited from information provided by my former colleague Kim Hyun (Seoul National University).

collocations (compare with *Happy New Year* in English). There should however not be any possible scientifically grounded objection if the tensification process itself and its domain of application were sufficiently understood.

In the present state of research, the phonetic and acoustic correlates of Korean tense consonants are still debated, and it is likely that tensification takes various forms depending on its locus of occurrence. It would be wiser to await further phonetic studies, and see if there is a continuum of tensification at word boundaries depending on the frequency of cooccurrence of these words. For instance, check if the imperative *pok patuseyyo* is a better locus for tensification than *pok patasseyo* '(I) got (was blessed with) happiness'.

The influence of semantics should also be taken into account, as the risk of ambiguities (loss of meaning contrast) may well forbid tensification to occur, e.g. 사다 *sata* 'buy' with tensification would take on 싸다 *ssata* 'cheap'. But as Martin (1992: 31) notes, "[T]he string / yakpalle/ can represent both *yak palle* 'applies medicine' and *yak-palle* 'is shrewd and quick'" (respectively from *yak.(ul) palle* 'medicine.(Obj) apply' and *yak.(ko) ppalle* 'shrew.Con quick'). Martin apparently includes tensification among the rules that "take place across words and phrases, when the phonetic cues to their boundaries are omitted, as often happens in normal rapid speech" (1992: 32).

No decisive conclusion can therefore be drawn about the maximal domain of application of phonological rules in Korean.

Testing the allophonic realizations [l] or [r] of the Korean phoneme /l/, Jun S.A. suggests that the domain of resyllabification "*can* occur accross any word boundaries within an Intonational Phrase".[64] This is probably the case for all processes that were mentioned above. In other

64 "In Korean, /l/ only surfaces in a coda position, unless it is part of a geminate. By /l/-Flapping, /l/ becomes a flap, [r] intervocally and is realized as an onset to the following syllable. [...] In the pilot study, I examined the domain of /l/-Flapping, using five sentences. Each sentence had an object NP ending in /l/ and a verb beginning with a vowel. [...] The results show that resyllabification *can* occur accross any word boundaries within an Intonational Phrase. [...] Thus, I assume that any coda can be resyllabified to be the onset of the initial syllable of the following Accentual Phrase, provided the Accentual Phrase is vowel-initial." (Jun S.A. 1995: 242)

terms, it is certain that they occur not only in compounds but also in free sequences. The only difference could eventually be stated in terms of whether they *must* occur in compounds while they *can* occur in free syntactic formations. As far as subject-predicate collocations are concerned, they would surely behave unlike typical compounds (such as noun-noun compounds). In the same way as their internal constituents can be separated by grammatical markers or even by other lexical elements (see the following section 2. 2, p. 139), the boundary between the subject and the predicate is also more likely to be the locus of a pause, thus to rule out phonological processes that would occur otherwise (save cases of anticipation).

2) Non-automatic tensification: epenthetic *s* and compounds

The process of "automatic" tensification of plain constituents occurring after obstruents was mentioned above. There is also a process of non-automatic, or irregular, tensification, that can be observed after non obstruent consonants, namely the lateral /l/ and the nasals /m/, /n/, /ng/.

This phenomenon is also referred to as "Bindung-s", or "*sai-sies*" (literally "in between-s", from the name of the letter <ㅅ> /s/ in Korean), as if there were an epenthetic *s*, the neutralization of which (to the corresponding plain alveolar stop /t/ in final position) triggers the tensification of a following plain consonant in the same way as seen above.

Positing an 's' epenthesis is justified on historical grounds, because there was a former genitive <ㅅ> 's' marker which is still spelled in compound words when the first word has, in isolation, a vocalic coda. See for instance the occurrence of *pi* 'rain, in the following compound:

(131) 비 *pi* 'rain' + 물 *mwul* 'water' → 빗물 *pi-s+mwul* [pi**n**.**m**wul]/ [pi**m**.**m**wul] 'rain water'

In this example, 's' is first neutralized to [t] because it is in the coda position, then assimilated to [n] or [m] because of the following nasal consonant. When 's' appears before a vowel, it is never realized as [s] but as [t] again:

(132) 위 *wi* 'upper' + 옷 *os* 'cloth' → 윗옷 *wi-s+os* [wi.tot] 'coat'

A similar *s*-epenthesis is also posited in contexts where the onset of the second element of a compound is tensed even though tensification is not expected to occur. Epenthetic *s* in such an environment has the same effect as a syllable final [t] on a following lax consonant, and in the same way, it may be considered as deleted due to the 'cluster simplification rule'. For instance:

(133) 위 *wi* 'upper' + 사람 *salam* 'person' → 윗사람 *wi-s+salam* [wi(s).**ss**alam] 'a senior'

(134) 산 *san* 'mountain' + 불 *pwul* 'fire' → 산불 *san-s+pwul* [san.**pp**wul] 'mountain fire'

The *s* epenthesis is an heritage from the past. Even though it may occur in newly formed words (by analogy?), its predictability in synchrony is still a matter of dispute among scholars. One general rule is that, in accordance with its former genitive function, it rather occurs in 'subordinate compounds' than in 'coordinate compounds' (Martin 1954, Kim C.W. 1970, Kim Y.S. 1985, Sohn H.M. 1999). Examples of both are given here:

(135) 봄 *pom* 'spring' + 바람 *palam* 'wind' → 봄바람 [pom.**pp**alam] 'spring wind'

(136) 물 *mwul* 'water' + 불 *pwul* 'fire' → 물불 [mul.**p**wul] (*[mwul.**pp**wul]) 'water and fire (= hardship)'

As a former genitive marker, Bindung-*s* is also not expected in synthetic compounds (formed of a verb and one of its arguments). However, given that (i) this *s* has lost its former grammatical function in modern Korean for a purely cohesive function in the realm of lexical formation, and (ii) genitive marking of subjects was once allowed in former stages of Korean,[65] there is no theorical reason to exclude the possibility that *s* could appear or have appeared between subjects and verbs as well.

A elicitation of several SPC providing an appropriate phonological context, shows however that irregular tensification, with or without *s*-epenthesis (cf. cases of vocalic hiatus), is not observed in subject-predicate collocations:

Context	[– epenthesis]	[+ epenthesis]
[m] + [p]	(Ø)	*pam-pap* [pam.**pp**ap] 'night-rice = night meal'
[n] + [p]:	*nwun-palkta* [nwun.**p**ak.tta] 'eye-clear = have good eyesight'	*nwun-pich* [nwun.**pp**it] 'color of one's eyes/of snow'
[ng] + [p]:	(Ø)	*simcang-pyeng* [sim.cang. **pp**yeng] 'heart-disease = heart disease'
[m] + [t]:	*cam-tulta* [cam.**t**ul.ta] 'sleep-enter = get sleepy'	*kum-tengi* [kum.**tt**eng.i] 'gold-lump = nugget of gold'
[n] + [t]:	*han-toyta* [ha:n.**t**oy.ta] 'spite-become = be sorry, regretful' *kanan-tulta* [ka.nan.**t**ul.ta] 'poverty-enter = be poor in'	*son-tocang* [son.**tt**o.cang] 'hand-seal = thumbprint'
[ng] + [t]:	*pyeng-tulta* [pye:ng.**t**ul.ta] 'sickness-enter = fall ill'	*kang-twuk* [kang.**tt**wuk] 'river-bank = riverbank'
[m] + [s]:	*kim-sayta* [ki:m.**s**ay.ta] 'steam-run_out = loose interest'	*palam-soli* [pa.lam.**ss**o.li] 'wind-sound = roar of the wind'
[n] + [s]:	*son-swipta* [son.**s**wip.tta] 'hand-easy = easy'	*nun-salam* [nu:n.**ss**a.lam] 'snow-man = snowman'
[ng] + [s]:	(Ø)	*kang-sok* [kang.**ss**ok] 'river-inside = in the river'
[m] + [c]:	*maum-cohta* [ma.um.**c**ot.tha] 'mind-good = good minded'	*mom-cip* [mom.**cc**ip] 'body-frame = stature, built'
[n] + [c]:	*kibun-cohta* [ki.pwun.**c**ot.tha] 'mood-good = feel good'	*son-cis* [son-**cc**it] 'hand-act = gesture'

65 Embedded subjects.

[ng] + [c]:	(Ø)	*tung-cwulki* [tung.**cc**wul.ki] 'back-line = line of the backbone'
[m] + [k]:	*kum-kata* [kum.**k**a.ta] 'crack-go = crack'	*pam-kil* [pam.**kk**il] 'night-road = night trip'
[n] + [k]:	*son-kata* [son.**k**a.ta] 'hand-go = take trouble' *son-kopta* [son.**k**op.tta] 'hand-numb = have numb hands'	*son-kapang* [son.**kk**a.pang] 'hand-bag = handbag, briefcase'
[ng] + [k]:	(Ø)	*tung-kacwuk* [tung.**kk**a.cwuk] 'back-leather = skin of one's back'
[n] + [c]:	(Ø)	*san-cwulki* [san.**cc**wul.ki] 'mountain-line = mountain range'
[l] + [p]:	*pwul-pwuthta* [pwul.**p**wut.tta] 'fire-stick = catch on fire'	*pal-patak* [pal.**pp**a.tak] 'leg-floor = sole of a foot'
[l] + [t]:	*paltal-toyta* [pal.tal.**t**oy.ta] 'development-become = develop' *mwul-tulta* [mwul.**t**ul.ta] 'water-enter = dye, take color' *nal-tulta* [nal.**t**ul.ta] 'day-enter = clear up' *mal-toyta* [ma:l.**t**oy.ta] 'word-become = make sense'	*pal-tung* [pal.**tt**ung] 'leg-back = instep of a foot'
[l] + [s]:	*nal-seta* [nal.**s**e.ta] 'edge-stand = become sharp' *kkol-sanapta* [kkol.**s**a.nap.tta] 'appearance-rough = shabby, ugly'	*nal-swu* [nal-**ss**wu] 'day-number = number of days'
[l] + [c]:	*kunul-cita* [ku.nul.**c**i.ta] 'shadow-become = get shaded' *kkol-cohta* [kkol.**c**o.tha] 'appearance-good = [...]'	*mal-caycwu* [mal.**cc**ay.ccwu] 'word-talent = eloquence'
[l] + [k]:	*simswul-kwucta* ['sim.swul.**k**wut.tta] 'cross_temper-bad = ill-tempered'	*pwul-kil* ['pwul-**kk**il] 'fire-road = flames, fire'

[i] + V:	*kwi-wulta* [kwi.wul.ta] 'ear-sing = have a singing in the ears' *wi-epsta* [wi.epta] 'above-not_exist = be the greatest'	

Such negative results had to be obtained and presented. They are consistent with the claim that synthetic compounds in general, including nominals derived from subject-verb sequences, do not undergo *s*-epenthesis (see Sohn H.M. 1986; Cho Y.M. 1994). Korean thus clearly differentiates from Japanese, which shows 'rendaku' applying to sub-compounds as well as to synthetic compounds (contrary to what is claimed in Sugioka 1984 and Vance 1987), though in a non-systematic way.

As a final remark, it is noteworthy that the main hint for phonological integration of noun-noun compounds, namely the *s*-epenthesis seen above,[66] is also a reminder of a former regular syntactic formation involving the insertion of a grammatical suffix. The exact equivalent in (subject) noun-verb compounds would be those found among type B SPC that displayed a fusion of the former subject suffix *i*. In other terms, the most frozen sequences from a morpho-phonological perspective are reminiscent of a very syntactic way of formation from a diachronic perspective.

3) Word-internal phonological processes and SPC

The phonological rules seen above apply to word boundaries, and, to the exception of *s*-epenthesis –which does not appear in SPC–, are observed at the boundary of phrases as well. Some of these rules also unconditionally apply within words, such as resyllabification.

Does this mean that there is no positive phonological clue as to the

66 One could also include the fewer N-N compounds with a reduced form of the genitive suffix *uy*, which was formerly restricted to animate possessions, as in 달걀 *talkyal* 'chicken egg', from 닭의 알 *talk.uy al* 'chicken.Gen egg'.

compound status of SPC in Korean?

The only positive clue among the data that could be gathered concerns two very frequent SPCs: *mas-issta* 'tasty' and *mes-issta* 'stylish'.

According to the neutralization rule applying to consonantal codas, the final [s] of a word is neutralized to the homorganic plain stop [t] if the word is followed by a pause or by another word. This process is illustrated in the following example with the SPC *mas-epsta* 'tasteless':

(137) 맛없다 *mas-epsta* 'taste-not_exist = tasteless' [ma.**t**ep.tta] (*[ma.sep.tta])

[s] pronunciation is however retained before the existential verb *issta* 'exist':

(138) 맛있다 *mas-issta* 'taste-exist = tasty' [ma.**s**i.tta] (also: [ma.ti.tta]?)

The "neutralized" pronunciation [ma.**t**i.tta] is also recorded as an alternative pronunciation in Korean dictionaries (also for 멋있다 *mes-issta* 'taste/flavour-exist = stylish, chic'). The non-neutralized pronunciation is however the most commonly, if not exclusively, heard one.

This exception to the neutralization rule is not accounted for in the works that were consulted, and it would stand as an exception, irrespective of whether the sequence is considered a free sequence or a compound.[67]

The behaviour of *issta* takes on that of the copula 이다 *ita* 'be' in the same context, as the [s] pronunciation would also be observed in 그 맛이다 *ku mas-ita* '(It) is this taste' [ma.si.ta] (not *[ma.ti.ta]).[68] The resemblance ends here. *ita* will forbid neutralization with all nouns ending in /s/, while *issta* would trigger neutralization with most nouns

67 Cf. "neutralization takes place under all conditions in compounds" (Lee I.S. & Ramsey, 2000: 69)

68 No occurrence of a noun plus the copula can be considered as a frozen formation. It is the slot that allows the largest paradigmatic variation, and is indeed taken as a determining context for the class of nouns as a whole (cf. Lee H.B., 1989: 40).

(as long as the subject particle *-i* is not expressed). Compare (139) and (140):[69]

	[+existential verb]	[+copular verb]
(139)	맛있다 *mas-issta* 'taste-exist' [ma.**si**.**t**ta]/ [ma.ti.tta]	맛이다 [ma.**si**.ta]
	멋있다 *mes-issta* '*ib.*' [me.**si**.tta] / [me.**ti**.tta]	멋이다 [me.**si**.ta]
(140)	갓 있다 *kas issta* 'hat exist' [ka.**ti**.**t**ta]	갓이다 [ka.**si**.ta]
	벗 있다 *pes issta* 'friend exist' [pe.**ti**.tta]	벗이다 [pe.**si**.ta]

There is little doubt that the existence of non-neutralized forms of *mas-issta* or *mes-issta* are related to the frozenness of these SPC, as compared to the behaviour of random nouns in the same context.

Other phonological process would be worth investigating, but restrictions in terms of phonological context, or variability of realization within the speech community would probably not allow to draw general conclusions. For instance the reduction of the diphtong *yey* [ye] to *ey* [e] after any consonant would probably not occur at a word boundary, as it does within words (e.g. 가계 *kakyey* 'shop', pronounced [kakey], but 각 예 *kak yey* 'each example' is very unlikely to be [kak ey]). However, as instances of verbs beginning with *yey* are rare, there might not be any collocation displaying the favorable phonological context for this reduction process to take place.

2. Morpho-syntactic integrity

Let us now investigate one step further some morpho-syntactic properties of SPC with respect to their internal separability (cf. Lieber 1992): particle retention or deletion, adverbial insertion, and placement

69 Note that these test examples with *issta* sound artificial to Korean ears: they would rather add a subject suffix *–i* between the noun and the predicate.

of negation.

1) Subject particle deletion vs. retention

As already mentioned, SPC in Korean almost always allow their subject component to be either unmarked or overtly marked as a subject.[70] This seems to be a general rule, with only dubious exceptions.

A Korean informant however warned me that some SPC sounded unnatural with a subject particle. The few examples that were quoted included: 꼴좋다 *kkol-cohta* 'shape-good', 짓궂다 *cis-kwucta* 'act, behaviour + bad = cross, prankish', 좀먹다 *com-mekta* 'moth-eat = be moth-eaten', and 길들다 *kil-tulta* 'way-enter = get accustomed, get tame'.

Contrary to this claim, it was however relatively easy to find several examples of the last two SPC displaying a subject particle, as in the following:

(141) 길이 들때까지...
kil.i tu.l.ttay.kkaci
way.S enter.Adn:Fut.time.until
"Until (X) gets accustomed to (Y)"

(142) 실크벨벳이면 좀이 먹겠죠 (http://lovealot.tistory.com/4567)
silkhu.beylbeys.i.myen com.i mek.keyss.cyo
silk.velvet.Cop.if moth.S eat.Fut.TS:Pol
"If it is silk velvet, it could get moth-eaten."

As for the two first sequences, no example of with the subject particle could be elicited, but their status as SPC is disputable for the following reasons.

꼴좋다 *kkol-cohta*, literally 'shape-good', is actually frozen as a fixed idiomatic sentence to ironically mean 'It serves X right!', or, colloquially, 'This sucks!'. It thus behaves differently from other subject-predicate frozen sequences that are able to be the center of a larger construction.

70 Instances isolated under the 'Type B' category are not considered here.

If such phraseologisms can ultimately be considered as collocations as well, and even as being stored as words in a speaker's mental lexicon, they do not behave as words with respect to sentence formation: they are *sentences by themselves.*

The case of *cis-kwucta* 'act, behaviour + bad = cross, prankish', is less conclusive. In *cis-kwucta*, *cis-* could be seen as an intensifying prefix rather than as a subject noun. As a matter of fact, *cis-* surely carries the meaning 'very, thoroughly' in the following verbs: 짓개다 *cis-kayta* '*cis-* + knead = knead (strongly)', 짓찧다 *cis-ccihta* '*cis-* + pound = pulverize', 짓누르다 *cis-nwuluta* '*cis-* + push, press = weigh heavily on', 짓두들기다 *cis-twutulkita* '*cis-* + beat = hit several times', 짓씹다 *cis-ssipta* '*cis-* + chew = chew thouroughly, masticate', 짓밟다 *cis-palpta* '*cis-* + trample = trample on (carelessly)', 짓이기다 *cis-ikita* '*cis-* + beat = mash, squash'.[71] While this list of verbs is semantically homogenous, all examples referring to movements involving pressure from some body part, *kwucta* singles out as a stative verb, describing a human propensity that fits better as a predicate of the abstract noun *cis* 'act, deed, behaviour' (cf. also the same structure with 심술궂다 *simswul.(i) kwucta* 'ill-nature.(S) be_bad = be ill-natured' where *simswul* definitely is a subject noun). Furthermore, the expression 짓이 나다 *cis.i nata* 'cis.S arise = disport oneself (usually out of habit)' shows that *cis* can be used as a (formally marked) subject with another verb. Depending on whether *cis-kwucta* is interpreted as meaning 'very bad' or as '(one's) act (is) bad', *cis-* could equally be interpreted as a subject or as an intensifying prefix. Semantic considerations alone are not conclusive, but as the subject interpretation seems more appropriate for the reasons given above, it could be surmised that the impossibility to insert a subject particle may be due to the influence of the prefixed formations listed above.

All in all, SPC that undergo compulsory particle deletion are therefore few to none. Given that the few examples that were elicited belong to a hundred of SPC that were checked with my informant, their scarcity can be considered as significant enough to consider that

71 *cis-* in this intensifying sense also forms nominal derivatives out of nouns, as in 짓고생 *cis-kosayng* '(serious) trouble, hardship', 짓망신 *cis-mangsin* '(serious) disgrace, infamy', etc. It is evidently not a subject noun in such cases.

they are exceptions. Moreover, as outlined above, a deeper study may reveal that even these exceptions are subject to variation whithin the speech community, or that other factors can explain the impossibility of inserting a subject particle.

Thus, if one considers that, *by definition*, compounds should never allow any grammatical material to appear inside the compounded sequence, the conclusion would be that Korean predicative SPC can never be considered as compounds. Of course, one could assume that the same sequences behave as lexical formations (i.e., compounds) when they are unmarked and as syntactic constructions when they are marked. The loss of the subject particle is in itself not conclusive since it is often observed in non collocational sequences, and there is no change in referential meaning with or without this subject particle, so that such a discrimination does not make much sense. More crucially however, one has to consider the informative function of the subject particle. In free combinations, it mostly selects a particular referent out of a paradigm of competing subjects. In fixed combinations, such as SPC, the subject particle rather marks the rhematic integration of the subject into the main predicate. In other terms, it indirectly signals that the subject is not independent from its accompanying verb (see Chap. 3).

2) Adverb placement

Let us now check the separability of SPC with regard to adverbial modification. Irrespective of their belonging to one of the types listed above (minus Type B), SP collocations may allow two placement possibilities for adverbial modifiers:

(i) Subject(Y) Adv Verb
(ii) Adv Subject(Y) Verb

Pattern (ii) is not expected for non-collocational subject verb sequences when adverbs directly modify the predicate, especially adverbs of degree and manner. Copula clauses are an exception, because adverbs must always precede the complement of the copula.

Let us take two degree adverbs as a first illustration: *manhi* 'much, many', and *mopsi* 'very, exceedingly'. As can be seen from the following examples with pronominal arguments, *mopsi* rather appears just before the verb, therefore after the subject of the sentence. The subject can be an experiencer as in (143) or a stimulus subject as in (144). If two subjects are expressed, *mopsi* also naturally occurs after both subjects (145):

(143) 저 지금 **몹시** 무서워요! (www.msportal.net/blog/sau/91)
ce cikum mopsi mwuseweyo
P1 now very fear/scared
"I'm totally scared now!"

(144) 지금 그가 **몹시** 그립다 (spn.chosun.com/site/data/)
cikum ku.ka mopsi kulipta
now he.S very miss
"(I) miss him very much now."

(145) 난 니가 **몹시몹시** 싫어요. (trickworld.dataclub.net/me/6011561)
na.n ni.ka mopsi-mopsi silheyo
I.Top you.S very-very dislike
"I hate you."

This preferential placement usually also obtains with subject nouns referring to independent entities such as *palam* 'wind', or with relational subject nouns such as *iwus* 'neighbor' or *nwun* 'eye':

(146) 초새벽 바람이 **몹시** 차가웠다. ... (www.feedshow.com/)
cho.saypyek palam.i mopsi chakaw.ess.ta
early.dawn wind.S very cold.Past.TS
"The wind of early dawn was very cold."

(147) 그 이웃이 **몹시** 수상하다. (pdf.hallailbo.co.kr/sectionpdf/)
ku iwus.i mopsi swusanghata
this neighbor.S very suspicious/suspect
"This neighbor is very suspicious."

(148) 임신을 하고 출산의 과정을 거치면서 눈이 **몹시** 피로하고 나빠진 것 같습니다. (ksea.paran.com/sknow/queview.php)
imsin.ul ha.ko chwulsan.uy kwaceng.ul kechi.myense nwun.i mopsi philoha.ko nappaci.n.kes kathsupmnita
pregnancy.Obj do.Con delivery.Gen process.Obj pass_through.while eye.S very weary.Con go_bad.Adn thing seem.TS
"During pregnancy and birth, it seems that her eyes (= of the mother) were extremely weary and went bad."

In the case of SPC, constructions (i) may alternate with constructions (ii). This is true for SPC of type C (149), D (150-151), as well as A (meteorological clause in 152):

-*hwa.(ka) nata* 'anger-arise = get angry':
(149) 나 지금 화가 **몹시** 나있어. (www.i-rince.com/2512132)
na cikum hwa.ka mopsi na isse
I now anger.S very arise exist.TS
"Now I'm very angry."

한 부부가 부부싸움을 하다 남편이 **몹시** 화가 났다. (blog.daum.net/nyy9858/)
han pupu.ka pupu.ssaum.ul ha.ta namphyen.i mopsi hwa.ka na.ss.ta
one couple.S couple.fight.Obj do.Con very anger.S go_out.Past.TS
"One couple had a quarrel, and the husband got very angry."

-*mas.(i) nata* 'taste_arise = be tasty':
(150) 사서 먹는 김치 조미료 맛 **많이** 나잖아요 (dnshop.daum.net/)
sa.se mek.nun kimchi comilyo mas manhi na.canha.yo
buy.Con Eat.Adn kimchi seasoning taste much arise.TS.Pol
"(It) tastes a lot like the chemical seasoning of the kimchi we buy (in stores) [and eat], you know."

우리나라서 먹는 파파야보다 **많이** 맛나더라구요... (www.indofantazy.com/)
wuli nala.se mek.nun phaphaya.pota manhi mas.na.te.lakwu.yo
our country.Loc eat.Adn papaya.than much taste.arise.Retr.Quot.Pol
"[I remember] (they) are much more tasty than the papayas (we) eat in our country."

-pay.(ka) kophuta 'belly-hungry = hungry':

(151) 그는 이제서야 배가 **굉장히** 고프다는 걸 깨달았다. (Harry Potter 1)
ku.nun iceyseya pay.ka koyngcanghi kophu.ta.nun ke.l kkaytal.ass.ta
he.Top now belly.S very hungry.Quot.Adn:Pres Nom.Obj realize.Past.TS
'He just realized that he was very hungry.'

나 몹시 목말랐거든.. 먼저 주문할까? 나 **굉장히** 배고파 (reportworld.co.kr)
na mopsi mok.malla.ss.ketun.. mence cwumwunha.l.kka? na koyngcanghi pay.koph.a
I very throat.thirsty.Past.TS.. first order.Fut.Q? I very belly.hungry.TS
'I was very thirsty. Can we order first? I'm so hungry.'

-pi.(ka) ota 'rain-come = rain':

(152) 요즘 비가 **많이** 와서 고추를 못 말린대요. (kr.blog.yahoo.com/ywook5730/)
yocum pi.ka manhi wa.se kochwu.lul mos malli.n.tay.yo
these_days rain.S much come.Cause pepper.Obj Neg dry.Past.Quot.Pol
"They say that they couldn't dry the peppers because it rained a lot these days."

그동안 **많이** 비와서 무공수련을 못 한 것도 [...]. (www.tennisnara.com/board/)
ku_tongan manhi pi.wa.se mukongswulyen.ul mos ha.n.kes.to
meanwhile much rain.come.Cause military_action.Obj Neg do.Adn.thing.Also
"Also the fact that in the meantime, (they) couldn't distinguish themselves in action because it rained a lot."

As can be seen from the examples above, the same sequences may allow both the S-Adv-P order and the Adv-S-P order. One factor that seems to influence the choice of the first order, the one which is generally observed in free sequences, is the presence of a functional expansion of the noun element of the SPC. In the following sentence, the noun *kiek* 'memory' is modified by a genitive phrase specifying the content of the memory, that is, a memory of the 'White Pension'. The frequency adverb *cacwu* 'often' is placed directly before the verb *nata* 'arise':

(153) 지난 여름때 묵었던 "화이트펜션"의 기억이 자주 나네요. (local.naver.com)
cinan yelum.ttay muk.ess.te.n hwaithu.peynsyen.uy kiek.i cacwu na.ney.yo
last summer.time stay.Past.Retr.Adn white.pension.Gen memory.S often arise.TS
"The memory of the 'White Pension' (I) stayed at last summer often comes (to my mind)."

The superlative adverb *kacang* 'most' is however preposed to the whole sequence in the following example, in which nothing modifies the noun:

(154) 라이온킹~가장 기억나는 명장면!! (http://cafe.daum.net/shiki4ever)
laion.khing ***kacang*** *kiek.na.nun myengcangmyen*
lion.king **most** memory.come_out.Adn:Pres scene
"Lion King~The scene I remember most!"

The possibility for the noun constituent to be modified independently is actually taken as a hint that the sequence is not a compound. Both orders may however be observed even in cases in which the noun cannot take any modifier. This alternative is illustrated by the following contrast with the sequence *him-tulta* 'energy-enter = tired/tiring':

-*him.(i) tulta* ('energy-enter = get tired/tiring'):

(155) 보통날보다 무거운 배낭때문인지 힘이 **몹시** 들었다. (suramalpine.com)
pothong nal.pota mukewu.n paynang.ttaymun.i.nci him.i mopsi tul.ess.ta
usual day.than heavy.Adn knapsack.because.Cop.whether energy.S very enter.Past.TS
"Maybe because (my) knapsack was heavier than usual, I got very tired."

(156) 남성 팬들이 **몹시** 힘들어 한다?! (news.korea.com/journal/read.asp)
namseng phayn.tul.i mopsi him.tul.e_ha.n.ta
male fan.Plur.S very energy.enter.Pres.TS
"Male fans are suffering very much?!"

Some SPC seem to be more integrated than others, so that an adverb such as *elmana* 'how much', here in an exclamative interpretation, is more naturally placed before the whole sequence:

-*sok-sanghata* 'inside-be_hurt = feel bad, worry':

(157) 부모님이 얼마나 속상하시겠어요 (Drama, MBC, 080123, 8:40)
pumonim.i elmana sok.sangha.si.keyss.e.yo
parents.S how_much inside.be_hurt.Hon.Fut.Lnk.TS
"How worried must (your/their) parents be!"

-sin-nata 'joy, delight-arise = get excited':

(158) 첫눈도 맞고,, 얼마나 신나던지,,, (SSH, 29/11/2007, 17h56)
ches.nwun.to mac.ko elmana sin.na.te.n.ci
first.snow.also be_exposed_to.Con how joy.arise.Ret.Adn.whether
"How excited I got when I met the first (flakes of) snow!"

3) Preverbal negation

There are two main ways of negating a verbal predicate in a Korean assertive sentence. In one, the so-called short-form negation, the negative adverb *an(i)* is placed directly before the predicate, as in:

(159) 아유~ 너 하나도 안 변했다. (www.kyunggi.or.kr/bbs/view.php)
ayu~ ne hanato an pyenhay.ss.ta
you not_one Neg change.Past.TS
"You haven't change a bit."

(160) 뭐 답변도 하나도 안 합니까?? (uiseong.go.kr/.../free_board/Default.aspx)
mwe tappyen.to hanato an ha.pnikka
what reply.too not_one Neg do.Q
"Don't (you/they) even reply?"

As shown in these two examples, *an* cannot be separated from the verb by another syntactic constituent such as *hanato* 'one.also = (here) [not] even one', or by a subject or an object.

The long-form negation, on the other hand, is a postverbal one: the suffix *-ci* attaches to the verb stem and this infinite verb form is followed by the negative verb *anhta*, which is the contraction of the negation *an* plus the anaphoric verb *hata* 'do':

(161) 녹차는 임산부에게 나쁘지 않습니다. (http://judong.co.kr/wedding/70290)
nokcha.nun imsanpu.eykey nappu.ci_anh.supnita
green_tea.Top pregnant_woman.Dest bad.Neg.TS
"Green tea is not bad for pregnant women."

When short-form and long-form negations can alternate, the latter is refutative (e.g. 'It is not as you think'), but these two forms cannot alternate freely. For instance, the copula of an attributive sentence whose main predicate is a noun should be negated by the short-form only. Also, as noted by Sohn H.M. (1999: 391), adjectives rather take the long form while "adjectives of three or more syllables usually are not acceptable in short forms. Thus, for instance *alumtap-ci an-h-ta* 'be not beautiful' is natural while *an alumtap-ta* is not". This points to a categorial constraint, i.e. bearing on a particular part of speech (adjectival verbs), and, within this part of speech, a phonological constraint concerning the length of the negated constituent.

Moreover, there is a preference for the long-form negation over the short-form when the verb is a "compound one" (Sohn H.M. 1999):

> "[...] when the verb is a compound one, as in *konpu-hata* (study-do) 'study', *yath-pota* (low-see) 'look down upon', and *nal-ttwita* (fly-jump) 'act violently', long-form negation is preferred to short-form negation, as in *konpuha-ci an-h-nun-ta*[72] and *yathpo-ci an-h-nun-ta*, but not **an kongpuha-n-ta* and **an yathpo-n-ta*. If, however, a compound verb is separable, a negative adverb can be placed between the component elements, as in *kongpu (lul) an ha-n-ta* 'does not study'. Compound adjectives cannot be separated in this way, as in **hayngpok an ha-ta* 'be not happy'." (Sohn H.M. 1999: 391)

72 The notation adopted by Sohn H.M. segmenting the negative morpheme *an-* on the one hand, and *h-* (from *ha-ta* 'do') on the other, makes it clear that the negative sequence (*-ci*) *anh-ta* is originally a short-form negation operating on an anaphoric verb. However, on morphological grounds, *anh-ta* can be considered as an independent negative verb: the thematic vowel it selects before some suffixes is –very regularly– an '*a*', whereas *ha-ta* 'do' is irregular (see *ha-ci_anh.**a**.yo*'doesn't do' vs. *an-h**a.y**.yo anh.**a**.yo*'doesn't do').

In this context, SP collocations are expected to take the long-form negation or the short-form occurring directly before the verb constituent. This possibility is illustrated in:

(162) 기분이 안 좋다. (*City*, 08.02.15, 1)
*kipwun.i **an** coh.ta*
mood.S Neg good.TS
"(I) feel bad."

However, a few instances of SPC were recorded that display the short-form negation before the noun constituent. Our data includes *kep-nata* 'fear-arise = get scared', *sin-nata* 'joy-arise = get excited', *sayngkak-nata* 'thought-arise', *ccacung-nata* 'fret-arise = fretful, irritate', or *pi-ota* 'rain-come = rain', as in the following data found on the web:

(163) 에이즈는 안 겁나? (dramajeju.pe.kr/html/drama/baikal03.html)
*aicu.nun **an** kep.na*?
AIDS.Top Neg fear.arise:Lnk
"Don't you fear AIDS?"

(164) 맨끝에 신나잖어? 안 신나? (www.cine21.com)
*mayn.kkuth.ey sin.na.canhe // **an** sin.na*
most.end joy.arise.TS Neg joy.arise:Lnk?
"At the very end it's exciting, you know? Is it not exciting?"

(165) 아무리 생각해내려고 해봐도 잘 안 생각나. (blog.nomad21.com)
*amwuli sayngkakhay.nay.lyeko hay.pw.a.to cal **an** sayngkak.na*
however think.take_out.Intention do.see.Lnk.also well Neg thought.arise:Lnk
"No matter how (hard) I try to think of it, I just can't."

(166) 안 짜증나! 짜증 안나는 파파가 될테니까, (gyaru00.tistory.com/tag/득구)
an *ccacung.na! ccacung an na.nun phapha.ka toy.l.they.nikka*, [...]
Neg fret.arise:Lnk fret Neg arise.Adn:Pres daddy.S become.Adn:Fut.Con
"I'm not irritated! As I'll be a daddy that doesn't get irritated, ..."

(167) 비가 내려도 엄마, 지금 안 비와? (mothernbaby.com)
pi.ka naylye.to emma, cikum ***an*** *pi.w.a? ilehkey mwul.e po.pnita*
rain.S come_down.also mum, now Neg rain.come.Lnk // this_way ask.Lnk see.TS
"Even if it rains... mummy... Doesn't it rain now? [...]"

Moreover, contrary to Sohn's expectations, even adjectival SPC may display this behavior. This is illustrated in (168) with a sequence formed by the noun *pay* 'belly' and the adjectival verb *kophuta* 'hungry':

(168) 혜규야. 안배고파?? (my.dreamwiz.com/doolye/student2000/1609_16.htm)
hyeykyu.ya ***an*** *pay.koph.a*
Hye-Gyu.Address Neg belly.hungry.Lnk
"Hey Hye-Gyu, ain't you hungry?"

The following illustrates other SPC that have adjectival properties although the verb constituent is not originally an adjectival verb (= subgroup of Type D):

-mas-issta 'taste-exist = tasty':

(169) 그래 맛있겠지, (오복 보며) 어떤 꽃겐데 안 맛있겠냐? (kbs.co.kr/drama/)
kulay mas.iss.keyss.ci, (opok po.mye) etten kkochkey.ntey ***an*** *mas.iss.keyss.nya*

be_so taste.exist.Fut.TS, (O-Bok see.while) what_kind flower.crab.Con Neg taste.exist.Fut.Q
"Sure, it'll be tasty, (looking at O-Bok) what kind of blue crab wouldn't be tasty?" [= How would blue crab not be tasty?]

-sayk-taluta 'color-different = strange, peculiar':

(170) 나두 저번주에 다른 곳에서 동수샘 봤는데 ... 별루 안 색달라 보이던데 ㅋㅋ. (www.m-academy.org/bbs/view.php)
na.twu cepen cwu.ey talun kos.eyse tongswu.saym pw.ass.nuntey ... pyellwu ***an*** *sayk.tall.a po.i.te.ntey*
I.also this week.Temp other place.Loc Tongsoo.prof see.Past.Con ... particularly Neg color.different.Lnk see.Pass.Ret.Con
"This week I've also seen Pr. Tongsoo in another place. He didn't look particularly strange"

-him-tulta 'energy-enter = tired/tiring':

(171) 토요일 날에 혼자 가니 안힘 듬니까 [그러길래 같이 갔어야죠] (www.bccc.or.kr/bbs/view.php)
thoyoil nal.ey honca ka.ni ***an*** *him.tu.mnikka [...]*
saturday day.Temp alone go.Con Neg energy.enter.TS:Q
"As you've been (there) alone on Saturday, isn't it hard? [...]."

-caymi-issta 'fun-exist = funny':

(172) 그다지 사진 찍는게 별로 안 재밌었기 때문이죠...^^;; (jubaristudio.tistory)
kutaci sacin ccik.nun.ke.y pyello ***an*** *caymi.ss.ki_ttaymwun.i.c.yo*
that_much photo take.Adn.thing.S particularly Neg fun.exist.because.Cop.TS.Pol
"You know, it's because taking pictures isn't particularly funny."

Complex predicates, and among them complex adjectival sequences incorporating a subject, thus allow preverbal negation to appear before the noun. This holds as well for complex predicates formed with *hata* 'do' and a noun constituent functioning as an object, such as *kekceng-hata* 'worry-do = worry' in this example:

(173) 안 걱정 해도 되구요. (www.fulssi.or.kr/bbs/zboard.php)
an *kekceng hay.to toy.kwu.yo*
Neg worry do.also become.Con.Pol
"It's alright even if [you] don't worry = You don't have to worry."

Sohn's statement should thus be positively rephrased, because the pattern he excludes for compound verbs or adjectival verbs in general is actually observed. It is also true that this is not a common pattern. Only few instances were found, and they are mostly observed in a refutative use, that is contradicting another statement involving the positive counterpart. Their semantic interpretation is thus close to what was advocated for the long-form negation as opposed to the (regular) short-form negation.

Some complex predicates may thus oppose three different negative patterns: (i) a short-form negation before the verb constituent, (ii) a short-form negation before the noun constituent, and (iii) a postposed long-form negation. Obviously, pattern (ii) takes on the syntactic pattern in (i) because it is a short-form, but resembles more (iii) in semantic terms. There might be a difference in use between (ii) and (iii), as pattern (ii) could be specifically used in contexts where the positive complex predicate is conjointly uttered. Examples (165, 166, 168 and 170) precisely have a positive counterpart in the preceding clause: *sin.na.canh.e* "It's exciting, you know", *sayngkakhay.nay* "[no matter how hard I try to] think of it", *pi.ka naylye.to* "even if rain comes down", *mas.iss.keyss.ci* "It'll be tasty for sure". These sequences are even presupposed rather than asserted. This makes the use of negation more controversial, and in such a marked context, the use of the regular long-form negation may well be felt as weaker. Its 'contrary-to-one's-expectation' meaning is also lost in many of its uses (e.g. with polysyllabic adjectival verbs).

Nevertheless, in syntactic terms, Subject Predicate Collocations allowing short-form negation before their noun constituent demonstrate a behavior expected from single predicates only, so that they could be seen, in that respect, as compound words.

3. Functional hints to wordhood: categorial change

This section will consider functional properties of the whole SP sequence that cannot be derived from any of the two constituents. The fact that a given complex sequence displays specific properties, in terms of categorial status or of functional expansion, points to an autonomous behavior and thus to a greater integration of this sequence. One should however be cautious in considering these acquired properties as specific to words.

1) Translation to adjectival verb

A subgroup of SPC was classified as adjectival verbal complexes because they are intrinsically gradable (Type D). This property was tested by inserting them in a comparative construction, in order to see whether or not they need the presence of an adverb such as *te* 'more' or of another adverb.

Simple non-descriptive verbs are not supposed to display this property. In other terms, verbs that are not intrinsically gradable, such as *walk* or *sing*, cannot *directly* refer to a relative quantity of their arguments with respect to a comparative element. Since a sentence containing *than* is ungrammatical in English without a comparative adjective and adverb, one has to constrast the behaviour of adjectives and verbs using the analytic sequence 'compared to':

(174) ✓*Compared to Tara, Mike is lazy.*

(175) **Compared to Tara, Mike walks.*

(176) ✓*Compared to Tara, Mike walks a lot/more / fast(er) / (more) often.*

Only the presence of an adverb makes the verbal clause felicitous with a comparative element, whereas with a (gradable) adjectival clause, the quality referred to is naturally interpreted as being in a relatively bigger "quantity".

The following illustrates similar phenomena in Korean with the intransitive verbs *issta* 'exist, there is', *nata* 'arise', or *ota* 'come':

(177) *이전보다 차가 있어.
icen.pota cha.ka iss.e
before.Comparative car.S exist.Lnk
(Lit.) "There are cars compared to before." (intended: 'There are more cars than...')

(178) *이전보다 길이 났어.
icen.pota kil.i na.ss.e
before.Comparative road.S arise.Past.Lnk
(Lit.) "Roads appeared compared to before." (intended: 'There are more roads than...')

(179) *어제보다 비가 왔어.
ecey.pota pi.ka w.ass.e
yesterday.Comparative rain.S come.Past.Lnk
"Rain came compared to yesterday." (intended: 'It rained more than...')

For these sentences to become grammatical, one should either add an adverb or change the predicate. The first sentence, for instance, would have to be changed to *icen.pota cha.ka manhi isse* (before.Comparative car.S a_lot exist) or, more naturally, to *icen.pota cha.ka manha* (before. Comparative car.S be_many).

Yet, with the first two intransitive verbs –*issta* 'exist' and *nata* 'arise'[73]–, some subject predicate sequences are natural without any additional marking. For example:

73 I could not elicit such an example with *ota* 'come'.

(180) 그들의 밤은 우리의 낮보다 재미있어? (kjlab.com/bbs/view.php)
ku.tul.uy pam.un wuli.uy nac.pota caymi.iss.e
3P.Plur.Gen night.Top we.Gen day.Comparative fun.exist.Lnk
"Is/Are their night(s) funny compared to our day(s)?"

(181) 삼겹살이 소고기보다 맛나다 (http://blog.daum.net/maehok/7372993)
samkyepsal.i sokoki.pota mas.na.ta
Samgyeopsal.S beef.Comparative taste.arise.TS
"Samgyeopsal [grilled pork] is tasty compared to beef."

Other sequences, with *tulta* 'enter' or *epsta* 'not_exist', can be contrasted as well:

(182) ✓이전보다 힘들었어.
icen.pota him.tul.ess.e
before.Comparative energy.enter.Past.Lnk
"It was more tiring than before."

(183) *이전보다 돈들었어.
icen.pota ton.tul.ess.e
before.Comparative money.enter.Past.Lnk
"It cost more than before."

(184) 전 결혼식보다 정신없더라고요. (http://cafe451.daum.net/_c21_/bbs_search_read)
cen kyelhonsik.pota cengsin.eps.te.lako.yo
I.Top marriage_ceremony.Comparative mind.not_exist.Ret.Quot.Pol
"I tell you, I was more out of my mind than during the ceremony."

(185) (*)이전보다 나무가 없어.
icen.pota namu.ka eps.e
before.Comparative tree.S not_exist
"There are less trees than before."

The degree of acceptability may vary in some cases. For instance, as mentioned above, *kwi.ka mekta* 'ear.S eat = get deaf' is weird in the comparative without an additional adverb:

(186) (?)평범한 사람들보다 (더) 귀가 먹었다.
phyengpemha.n salam.pota kwi.ka mek.ess.ta
normal.Adn people.Plur.Standard ear.S eat.Past.TS
"(He) is deafer than normal people."

But it is far better than *mekta* 'eat' in its canonical sense:

(187) *한국사람은 일본사람보다 김치 먹지.
hankwuk.salam.un ilpon.salam.pota kimchi mek.ci
Korean.people.Top Japan.people.Comparative eat.TS
(Lit.) "Koreans eat kimchi compared to the Japanese, for sure."

It should now be observed that the subject nouns are not, by themselves, compatible with a marker of comparison, whether alone (e.g., as for a book title), or within a copular clause:

(188) *어제보다 재미
ecey.pota caymi
yesterday.Comparative fun
(Lit.) "The fun/interest compared to yesterday."

(189) *어제보다 재미다.
ecey.pota caymi.Ø.ta
yesterday.Comparative fun/interest.(Cop).TS
(Lit.) "It is fun compared to yesterday."

The line of argumentation goes like this. Since both (i) the verbal predicate alone, due to its semantics, and (ii), the subject noun, because of its nominal status, cannot be directly built with a standard of comparison, the fact that their combination acquires this property, shows that a new linguistic unit has come into being.

Another consequence of this newly acquired gradability is, for a subset of tokens, the ability to enter the colloquial and idiomaticized pattern Verb-*e(se)* + *cwukkeyss-*.[74] *cwukkeyss-* is composed of the verb stem of *cwukta* 'die' and the futuritive/modal suffix *-keyss-*. *-e*, or *-ese*, is a converbal suffix indicating the cause of the event. The whole pattern thus literally reads as 'be going to die because of (verb)', but metaphorically as an expression of high degree, e.g.:

(190) 더워서 죽겠다
tew.e.se cwuk.keyss.ta
hot.Link.Cause die.Fut.TS
"The heat is killing me."

As can be seen from the example, the logical subject of *cwukta* 'die' –in a metaphorical reading– is always understood as ego ('I') in plain assertive sentences. This is because the construction implies a strong subjective feeling toward external stimuli or situations. Typical verbs entering this construction include: *cohta* 'good/like', *mipta* 'bad/dislike' *tepta* 'hot', *chwupta* 'cold', *kwichanhta* 'annoying', *simsimhata* 'bored/boring', *phikonhata* 'tired', *aphuta* 'sick, hurt', *michita* 'mad', *wuskita* 'ridiculous', *changphihata* 'ashamed, embarrassed', *kwungkumhata* 'wonder', etc. In comparison, the canonical uses of verbs like *issta* 'exist' or *nata* 'arise' cannot occur together with *cwukkeyss-*. Yet, SPC with these verbs may again behave as gradable descriptive verbs, e.g.: *mas-issta* 'taste-exist = be tasty', *hwa.ka nata* 'anger.S arise = be angry', or *ccacung-nata* 'fret-arise = feel irritation':[75]

74 This second property seems highly language-specific. It has still to be worked out whether comparable constructions exist in other Asian languages.

75 Also with other argument-predicate collocations, such as *suthuleysu patta* 'get stress'; *patta* 'get, receive' is also not inherently gradable.

(191) 된장찌게 맛있어 죽겠어~ (http://cufe.tistory.com)[76]
toyncang.ccikey mas.iss.e cwuk.keyss.e
(soybean) thick_sauce.stew taste.exist.Lnk die.Fut.TS
"(This) soybean stew is so good!"

(192) 이런 거 볼 때면 정말 화가 나 죽겠어. (http://k.daum.net/qna/file/view.html)
ilen ke po.l_ttay.myen cengmal hwa.ka na cwuk.keyss.e
such thing see.when.if really anger.S go_out.Lnk die.Fut.TS
"Whenever (I) get to see such things, I'm so angry!"

(193) 요즘 공부도 안 되고 짜증나 죽겠어. (http://k.daum.net/qna/file/view.html)
yocum kongpu.to an toy.ko ccacung.na cwuk.keyss.e
these_days study.also Neg become.Con irritation.go_out.Lnk die.Fut.TS
"These days (as) I also can't study well, I'm so pissed off!"

SPC of Type D were classified as adjectival complexes because of their inherent gradability. As SPC belonging to this group may contain a basically non-gradable verb, their newly acquired gradability should also be considered as a case of intracategorial shift from active verb to descriptive verb.

If the categorial status of a given linguistic unit is to be taken as a property of words, then these SPC have word properties.

This stance is however questionable, for reasons that have to be explained, because this has not been yet much investigated.

Changes in the categorial status of linguistic units have been described from the perspective of two different levels of segmentation. The first one is a well known field of investigation in linguistic description, and is referred to as 'derivational morphology'. Very commonly, derivational formations are processes by which a word

76 The word for 'stew' should be spelt 찌개 *ccikay*. The vowels 애 *ay* [ɛ] and 에 *ey* [e] are usually neutralized in Modern Korean, which often causes such mispellings.

is transformed into another word of a different category, e.g. *dancer* (noun) from *dance* (verb). This process usually requires a derivational morpheme, but words can also be derived without any segmental marking, as in *fish* (verb) from *fish* (noun) (cf. conversion or 'zero-derivation').

The second one pertains to what Tesnière (1959) named *translation* in French, and that, following Sangati & Mazza (2009), can be rendered as *transference* in English.[77] Transference is a syntax-oriented operation by which a lexical or syntactic unit is transferred from one syntactic category to another, usually by means of a grammatical morpheme, hence named *transferrer* (French *translatif*). The following examples illustrate transference processes respectively from adjective to substantive (194) by means of the transferrer *le* 'the', from substantive to adjective (195) by means of the transferrer *de* 'of' (or English *'s*), and from clause to adjective by means of the transferrer *que* (196) (From Tesnière 1959: 411, 443):

(194) *Le livre noir et* ***le*** *rouge*. ("The black book and **the** red [one]")

(195) *Le livre* ***d'****Alfred*. ("Alfred's book")

(196) *Le livre* ***que*** *j'ai lu*. ("The book which I have read")

The intracategorial shift from a 'non adjectival verbal complex' to an 'adjectival complex' could be treated as an instance of transference, even though there is no transferrer (i.e. no segmental mark dedicated to making a linguistic unit shift from one category to the other). As a matter of fact, this possibility was accounted for in Tesnière's work.[78] The examples of

77 The SIL glossary of terminology gives "transfer" (http://www.sil.org/linguistics/glossary_fe/).

78 "Il arrive que la translation ne soit marquée par rien. Dans ce cas, nous dirons que le marquant de la translation est zero (v. chap. 17), c'est-à-dire qu'il y a **translation sans translatif**. Mais il n'y en a pas moins translation. Signalé ou non par un marquant morphologique, le phénomène syntaxique reste le même. [...] L'existence de la translation sans translatif implique la condamnation de toutes les théories qui prétendent fonder la syntaxe sur la morphologie et ne reconnaître comme faits avérés

'zero-transference' he gives indicate a process not as productive as other, segmentally marked, transference processes,[79] but Tesnière's views of tranference encompass syntax and morphology, and he also discusses the case of compounds (Tesnière 1959: 406-408). Now if, as often thought, productivity is taken as a necessary feature of syntactic processes, then the process we are facing should be considered as a lexical matter. As it does not involve affixation, it is not a derivational process. It looks more like conversion in that it is neither productive nor predictable, and does not involve any additional segmental mark. The only difference lies in the fact that it affects two words instead of one.

Even if the process is thought to be of lexical nature, it does not discriminate purely lexical sequences from sequences that are explicitely marked as syntactic formations. In the example (192) above, or in the following instance, the subject noun is still marked by a subject particle:

(197) 왜 국산 맥주는 일본 맥주보다 맛이 없을까?
way kwuksan maykcwu.nun ilpon maycwu.pota mas.i eps.ul.kka
why national beer.Top Japan beer.Comparative taste.S not_exist.Adn:Fut.Q
"Why Korean beer is tasteless compared to Japanese beer, I wonder."

Once again, then, it is safer to assume that SPC are syntactic constructions that may behave as words, and hence are properly labelled as 'collocations'.

2) Complement clause selection

As part of their distributional properties, words have specific expansion

---

que ceux qui sont exprimés par un marquant morphologique [...]." (Tesnière, 1959: 380, 381)

79 Examples of zero-transference in the relevant chapter are all taken from French poorly productive combinations, e.g.: *un ruban orange* (from N to Adj); *la tour Eiffel* (from Proper N to Adj); *boire frais* (from Adj to Adv).

properties depending on their categorial status. For instance, a noun can be the head of a relative clause, but a verb cannot. Similarly a verb, descriptive or active, can introduce a complement clause, while most nouns cannot. In a study of support verb constructions, Hong C.S. & Lee S.H. (2003: 256) observe the expansion frames of the sequence 연락이 오다 *yenlak.i ota*, literally '(a) call come(s)'. They observe that two constructions are possible: one involves an attributive clause directly modifying the noun, the other introduces a quotation clause. The following illustrates their point:

(198) 학교에서 내게 [[합격했다는] 연락]이 왔다.
hakkyo.eyse nay.key [[*hapkyekhay.ss.ta.nun*] *yenlak*].*i w.ass.ta*
school.Abl I.Dest [[success.Past.Quot.Adn] call].S come.Past.TS
"There has been a call for you from the school (saying) that you passed (your exams)."

(199) ↔ 학교에서 내게 [[합격했다고] [연락이 왔다]].
hakkyo.eyse nay.key [[*hapkyekhay.ss.ta.ko*] [*yenlak.i w.ass.ta*]]
school.Abl I.Dest success.Past.Quot call.S come.Past.TS
"There has been a call for you from the school (saying) that you passed (your exams)."

Only in the first construction, they argue, the first constituent behaves as a noun, since it is modified by a 'relative' clause marked by the adnominal suffix *-nun*: 'the call that (you) passed your exams'. In the second sentence, the embedded quotation marker *-tako* serves as a complement clause for the complex predicate *yenlak.i ota* as a whole, as it would for any kind of verb of saying, including simple ones such as *hata* 'tell, do' or *allita* 'inform'. Note that *ota* 'come' alone cannot be attributed the responsibility for the selection of a quotation clause.

It is precisely the role of the nominal constituent in a support verb construction to act as a semantic predicate, bringing along its selectional restrictions. In other terms, the noun constituent is supposed to act as a noun in the first construction, and as a verb in the second one.

The first example is more conclusive than the second: indeed a clause marked by *-nun* is infelicitous if it is not headed by a constituent having a nominal status, whereas in many cases, *-tako* clauses cannot be said to be selected by a given constituent in a sentence. In other terms, the relation of quotation clauses with the main clause is rather loose, which is reflected by their incompatibility with a case marker. Let us consider the following example:

(200) 영어로 물어보니 모른다고 가버렸다. (www1.tourexpress.com/korea)
yenge.lo mulepo.ni molun.tako kapoly.ess.ta
English.Inst ask.Cause do_not_know.Quot leave.Past.TS
"When (I) asked (him/her) in English, (he/she said) "(I) don't know" (and) left."

It should be clear from this example that we cannot infer from the contiguity of a *-tako* clause with the main predicate that this predicate selects a quotation clause: *kapolita* 'leave' is not a verb of saying, and the *-tako* clause introduces a quotation without the help of any explicit introductory verb.[80]

There is thus no apparent reason to believe that *yenlak* 'call' in the previous sentence is responsible for the 'selection' of the quotation clause. To be conclusive, another proof that *yenlak* selects a *-tako* clause should be adduced.

In sentences such as (200), it would be possible to insert a connective form of a verb of saying (*hata* 'do, say') behind the complement clause and keep the same interpretation (201). When the main predicate is a verb of saying, such an insertion would give either a

---

80 Even the all-purpose verb *hata* 'do, say' may fail to integrate a quotation clause as a first interpretation. Trying to explain to my Korean friend that I had not disclosed my status as a professor when registering to a students club, I sent him the following message: 교수라고 안했어 *kyosu.lako an.hay.ss.e* (professor.(Cop).Quot Neg.*hata*). I failed in conveying the idea that '(I) hadn't said (I) was a professor', as the most natural interpretation for my friend was: 'Saying that (I) was a professor (= for this reason), (I) didn't do (it)'.

weird sentence, or result in a different interpretation, as if two different speech events had taken place, as in (202):

(201) 영어로 물어보니 모른다고 하고 가버렸다.
yenge.lo mulepo.ni molun.tako ha.ko kapoly.ess.ta
English.Inst ask.Con do_not_know.Quot say.Con leave.Past.TS
"When (I) asked (him/her) in English, (he/she) said "(I) don't know" (and) left."

(202) *학교에서 내게 합격했다고 하고 연락이 왔다.
hakkyo.eyse nay.key hapkyekhay.ss.ta.ko ha.ko yenlak.i w.ass.ta
school.Abl I.Dest success.Past.Quot say.Con call.S come.Past.TS
?"The school said that you passed, and a call came."

Contrast also the following two sentences:

(203) 나는 아버지께 고향으로 내려가겠다고 편지를 썼다. (book-shop.dnshop.com)
na.nun apeci.kkey kohyang.ulo naylye.ka.keyss.tako phyenci.lul ss.ess.ta
I.Top father.Dest hometown.Dir go_down.go.Fut.Quot letter.Obj write.Past.TS
"I wrote a letter to my father (saying) that I would go down home."

(204) 나는 아버지께 고향으로 내려가겠다고 하고 편지를 썼다.
na.nun apeci.kkey kohyang.ulo naylye.ka.keyss.tako ha.ko phyenci.lul ss.ess.ta
I.Top father.Dest hometown.Dir go_down.go.Fut.Quot say.Con letter.Obj write.Past.TS
"I said to my father that I would go down home and wrote a letter."

The sequence *yenlak.i ota* 'call.S come' thus seems to get a proper complementation pattern (a quotative complement clause) as the subject nouns loses its compatibility with an adnominal clause. Nevertheless, both patterns coexist. For other SPC, the picture is clearer and points toward a loss of expansion properties of the (subject) noun constituent, because it is usually difficult to modify the noun with an adnominal clause. Such is the case for SPC with an abstract subject, e.g. *him-tulta* 'energy-enter' or *kep-nata* 'fear-come out'. In addition such SPC may also go along with clauses that can be considered as genuine complement clauses.

Such is the case of clauses nominalized by *-ki*, which can be case-marked and have to be selected by specific verbal predicates.[81] The following illustrates two semantically homogenous sets of SPC and simple verbs behaving similarly with respect to *ki*-complementation: *kep-nata* 'fear-come_out = fear' vs. *musepta/twulyepta* 'fear' on the one hand, and *him-tulta* 'energy-enter = difficult, tiring' vs. *elyepta/pekepta* 'difficult' on the other:

(205) 업데이트하기가 겁납니다... (jobdahan.net/)
eptey'ithuha.ki.ka kep.na.pnita
update.Nm.S fear.come_out.TS
"I'm afraid to (launch) update(s)."

(206) 동맹들때문에 게임하기가 무섭다 (board.ogame2.kr/thread.php)
tongmayng.tul.ttaymwuney key'imha.ki.ka musepta
league.Plur.because_of game.Nm.S fearful
"Because of (the) alliances/leagues, I'm scared to play the game."

81 According to Lee K.D. (1993), *ki*-complement clauses refer to states-of-affairs that can be described as second order entities in Lyon's classification, that is, entities that take time and that can be said to "occur", rather than to be "true" or "false". Examples of predicates taking *ki*-complement clauses include *cohta* 'good', *kitalita* 'wait', *huimanghata* 'hope', etc.

(207) 부흥은 활동하기가 두려워요 (historykr.com/bbs/zboard.php)
puhung.un hwaltongha.ki.ka twulyewe.yo
revival.Top activity.Nm.S fearful.TS
"I fear to take part in the revival."[82]

(208) 블로그 하기가 넘 힘들다. (brainchaos.kr/213)
pulloku ha.ki.ka nem him.tul.ta
blog do.Nm.S very energy.enter.TS
"It's very difficult to make a blog."

(209) 자유게시판 등업하기가 어렵네... (anilife.co.kr/zbxe/)
cayu.keysiphan tungepha.ki.ka elyep.ney
freedom.notice_board upgrade.Nm.S difficult.ST
"It's difficult to upgrade [...]."

(210) 그런데 등장인물 생각하기가 영 버거워서 [...] (www.mrharrypotter.com)
kulentey tungcanginmul sayngkakha.ki.ka yeng pekewe.se
by_the_way character/cast think.Nm.S zero difficult.Con
"By the way/but, as thinking about the cast is not difficult at all [...]."

Given that the nouns (*kep* 'fear' or *him* 'energy') and the verbs *nata* 'appear' and *tulta* 'enter' cannot select a *ki*-complement clause, the selection of a *ki*-clause is a property of neither the subject constituent nor of the verb constituent of the respective SPC *kep-nata* 'fear' and *him-tulta* 'difficult'. It is rather a property of the whole sequence, which thus behaves as if it were a single word (e.g. *musepta* or *elyepta*) in having an argumental frame of its own.

According to the classification set forth in 1.3(p. 124), *kep-nata* is a collocation of Type C (non-gradable) while *him-tulta* belongs to Type D

82 The word *puhung* 'revival' probably refers to a group of prayers (*puhunghoy*) in Korean Protestantism.

(gradable SPC). Collocations describing natural phenomena (Type A) are not expected to be expanded by a complement clause, but fused forms such as Type B might have such a construction. Following is an example with *kuci-epsta* 'limitless':

(211) [...] Y 국민 학교는 여러 가지로 실망스럽기 그지없었다. (우리들의 일그러진 영웅)
[...] Y *kwukmin hakkyo.nun yele kaci.lo silmangsulop.ki kuci-eps.ess.ta*
Y national school.Top various sort.Inst disappointing.Nm end-not_exist.Past.FS
"[...] S Elementary School, for all sorts of reasons, was an enormous disappointment." (trans. K. O'Rourke)

Again, this change in selectional properties indicates that a given sequence behaves as simple words do, but does not lead to the conclusion that it is necessarily a compound.

For the sake of comparison, let us take an example from French.

The French locution *prendre garde* is composed of the verb *prendre* 'take' and the noun *garde* 'watch'. It means 'be careful, see not to do'. None of these constituents can, in isolation, take a finite clause introduced by *que* 'that' or an infinitive clause introduced by *à* 'to'. Yet *prendre garde* regularly introduces both complements. In the former case, it also governs the subjunctive mood:

(212) **prendre que* [+ complement clause] / *à* [+ infinitive]
**La/une garde que* [+ complement clause] / *à* [+ infinitive].

(213) *Prends donc garde que la lumière qui est en toi ne soit ténèbres*. (Luke, 11:35)
"Take heed therefore that the light which is in thee be not darkness." (King James Bible)

Prendre garde, compared to the simple verb *prendre*, surely has its own word-like properties in terms of complementation pattern, but considering it a compound (hence a word) would lead to the conclusion that French words can undergo internal flection: *nous pren-**ons**-garde*, *ils pren-**nent**-garde*, etc. This would be an unintuitive and contrary-to-fact statement. *Prendre garde* is, no doubt, a collocation with specific expansion properties and a word-like behaviour, but it is by no means a compound, and a similar claim be made for Korean *kep-nata* or *him-tulta*.

3

Conclusion

This chapter mostly brought negative evidence as to the compound status of Korean SPC. Properties that could be taken as hints for a greater integration are either non distinctive with respect to free sequences (as for most phonological processes), or conflicting with behaviors of identical sequences in other environments.

For instance, *mas-issta* 'taste-exist = be tasty' displays a highly unusual phonetic realization that is supposed to occur only in simple words, not even in compounds, and yet, as the greater number of Korean SPC, it can also show up with the subject particle attached to the nominal. Both such properties are sufficient to deny the compound status for *mas-issta*.

The tests of adverb insertion or negation placement gave apparently better results for several sequences. Indeed, the negation placement test may even lead to the conclusion that some SPC look more like simple words than genuine simple words (compare long adjectives with examples of SPC presented in 2.2.3), p. 148). Tests however also showed the versatility of SPC in terms of syntactic behavior: they may behave as simple words in one context, and as free sequences in another.

As concerns functional hints to wordhood, several examples were brought forth pointing to an autonomous behavior of several SPC with respect to their categorial identity as well as to their ability to govern their proper complements. But then again, this autonomous behavior cannot be naively taken as a proof of their wordness.

There is little doubt though that many properties disclosed in the course of this chapter support the idea that if SPC are not words, they show lexicalization effects. As syntactic combinations that supply the lexicon and share properties with lexical items, they are best treated as collocations (even though a few cases became fully lexicalized words in Modern Korean).

The main conclusion should however be stated as follows: lexicalization, or 'wordhood' in a wide sense, is *largely independent* from phonological, morphological, or syntactic frozenness.

This is a positive result that calls for an explanation. The next step will be made in the following chapter, where it will be claimed that wordhood is above all a problem of 'paradigmatic frozenness'.

Chap. 3

Paradigmatic Choice and the Margins of Syntax

1

Introduction: Optional arguments and argument-like adjuncts

It is a general rule, in Asian languages, though not in European languages, that functional equivalents of core arguments – subjects and objects – are optional, i.e. they can be left out without damage to the grammaticality of sentences.[1] Thus, they behave as what traditional grammar would call 'adjuncts'.[2] One should therefore consider that in these languages, there is no distinction between 'core arguments' and 'adverbial adjuncts' in terms of syntactic behavior, and that optionality is, for such languages, an ineffective means of classification.[3]

Leaving temporarily aside the problem of optionality, a distinction will be made between two types of constituents using the licensing – on these constituents– of particles indicating restriction ('only'), and addition ('also') as a test. Constituents able to fall under the scope of those two particles will be considered either to be arguments, or to be argument-like adjuncts, while those that do not will be seen as proper disjuncts. In line with claims made by a group of French descriptivist linguists, the tests applied here will allow to draw first a major demarcation line between two kinds of syntaxes: a micro-syntax corresponding to complements bound to the verb and to the assertive part of utterances, versus a macro-syntax more loosely linked. Then,

1 There are in fact exceptions.
2 See Park C.W. (2002) for a treatment of adjuncts.
3 Not satisfying either for European languages as well. For instance, many, if not most, transitive verbs in these languages also have intransitive uses. The other way round, a great deal of intransitive verbs may 'lose' their intransitivity, e.g. in so-called 'cognate object' constructions.

observing the behavior of collocational sequences with respect to the same diagnostic tests, a third syntactic level below 'micro-syntax' will be set up, namely a 'nano-syntax'.

The method employed is based on tests that are more reliable than the optionality criterium, especially for languages such as Korean, and also gives results that seem to match to a significant extent with structurally similar languages such as Mongolian, as well as for languages very different from Korean, i.e., English or French.

Let first explain the reasons that led to use these tests.

1. Some diagnostic tests for Spoken French (Groupe Aixois de Recherches en Syntaxe)

A French research team from Aix-en-Provence (*The Groupe Aixois de Recherche en Syntaxe / GARS*) devised a series of tools for the study of a particular spoken language (Spoken French). As the perspective of this team is basically descriptive, not theoretical, they focus on real data rather than on any a prioristic discourse on alleged language particulars or universals of structure. They also insisted that many traditional descriptive notions are ineffective when applied to spoken data, and strived to develop a more suitable means of description.

For instance, the traditional criteria of obligatoriness for distinguishing arguments from adjuncts is unsatisfactory. Indeed, if it were really applied, it would lead to count as adjuncts a great number, if not the majority, of direct and indirect objects. On the other hand, they observe that arguments, whether obligatory or not, display a set of properties that can be tested. They are as follows (see Blanche-Benveniste & al., 1990):

-Properties of arguments (and argument-like adjuncts)

a. Licensed in cleft constructions: Fr. *C'est* ... *qui/que* ... ('It is ... who/that')
b. Licensed under the scope of the negation marker: Fr. *ne* (V) *pas* ... ('not')

c. Licensed under the scope of the restriction marker: Fr. *ne* (V) *que* ... ('only')

These three properties are shared, for example, by the obligatory locative complement of the verb *aller* ('go'), as well as by the optional direct object of *manger* ('eat'):[4]

(214) *Il est allé {en Allemagne}*. "He went to Germany."
> *C'est {en Allemagne} qu'il est allé*. "It is to Germany that he went."
> *Il n'est pas allé {en Allemagne}*. "He didn't go to Germany."
> *Il n'est allé qu'{en Allemagne}*. "He only went to Germany."

(215) *Il a mangé ({une pomme})*. "He ate an apple."
> *C'est {une pomme} qu'il a mangée*. "It is an apple that he ate."
> *Il n'a pas mangé { une/de pomme}*. "He didn't eat an apple."
> *Il n'a mangé qu' {une pomme}*. "He only ate an apple."

To make sure that the scope of the restrictive or negative markers is precisely what is intended (here, the complement only), and not wider (for instance including the verb), one should see whether another complement of the same class can be put into contrast with the former, e.g., *Il n'est pas allé en Allemagne, mais en Suisse* "He didn't go to Germany, but to Switzerland".

It appears that elements that are not traditionally considered as arguments share the same properties. For instance, locative or temporal adjuncts, such as *en Suisse* "in Switzerland" in the following sentence, can enter cleft constructions and negative or restrictive constructions, with the same interpretation as above:

4 Curly brackets ('{}') in example sentences indicate a slot allowing paradigmatic variation.

(216) *Il a pris son petit-déjeuner {en Suisse}*. "He had his breakfast in Switzerland."
> *C'est {en Suisse} qu'il a pris son petit-déjeuner.*
"It is in Switzerland that he had his breakfast."
> *Il n'a pas pris son petit-déjeuner {en Suisse}, (mais {en Allemagne}).*
"He didn't have is breakfast in Switzerland, but in Germany."
> *Il n'a pris son petit-déjeuner qu'{en Suisse}, (pas {en Allemagne}).*
"He had his breakfast only in Germany, not in Germany."

2. The notion *rection large* (wide government)

As these adjunct constituents behave, save their syntactic optionality, as regular arguments, researchers of GARS have developed the notion *rection large* ('wide rection/government') (e.g. Blanche-Benveniste 1990, 2002), which incorporates not only constituents regarded as arguments, but also constituents regarded as adjuncts.

Naturally, this notion is meaningful if and only if other elements in a sentence behave differently. And so are elements that may be called "discourse constituents", or "disjuncts" as opposed to "adjuncts". Illustrations will be taken from English sentences, manipulating examples from Hasselgård, Johansson & Lysvåg (1999), but French would behave similarly:

-Adjuncts vs. disjuncts:
(217) *He first met {her in 1982}*. (time adjunct)
> *It is {in 1982} that he first met her.*
He wiped his hands {carefully} on the towel. (process adjunct)
> *It was {carefully} that he wiped his hands on the towel.*

(218) *Apparently, they never received your letter.* (modal disjunct)
> **It is {apparently} that they never received your letter.*
John said he couldn't help me, which is ridiculous. (comment disjunct).
> **It is {which is ridiculous} that John said he couldn't help me.*

While time or process adjuncts such as in (217) display argument properties, in terms of behavior with respect to cleft-formation, restriction, or negation, the modal and comment disjuncts do not. Moreover, "discourse constituents" are often seen as not "grammatically" integrated, but rather "pragmatically" or "prosodically", and are the ones usually left aside in grammatical description, especially in syntactic description. Indeed, given the difference in behavior with respect to the basic syntactic transformations used as tests, it may be claimed that such constituents are not governed by syntactic rules. However, with the help of tests, they may be integrated into grammatical description, albeit negatively. The GARS also coined new terminology that makes it clearer that these constituents should also constitute a target of syntactic description, in calling them "macro-syntactic" constituents, as opposed to "micro-syntactic" constituents (those pertaining to the wide government) (Berrendonner 1991; Blanche-Benveniste 2002). As already mentioned, the distinction can be roughly spelled out in terms of disjuncts on the one hand, versus adjuncts and arguments on the other.

"Macro-syntax"	*vs.*	"Micro-syntax"	
(macro-syntactic constituents)		(micro-syntactic constituents)	
≈ *Disjuncts/Discourse constituents*		≈ *Adjuncts*	≈ *Arguments*

3. Paradigmatic interpretation

While syntax has long been exclusively concerned with the *syntagmatic axis* (i.e. the question whether or not a given string of segments form a phrase, and if so, whether the syntagmatic structure fits with dependency relations), such approaches explicitly or implicitly highlight the *paradigmatic axis* (Deulofeu 2007). Indeed, the fact that micro-syntactic constituents such as subjects, objects, or place and time adverbials can generally be put into contrast with other constituents by means of negative, contrastive, exclusive, or restrictive markers (also questioned by means of interrogative proforms), shows that these constituents are the result of a paradigmatic choice on the part of the speaker. Discourse constituents, on the other hand, do not display these properties. In pragmatic terms, the distinction between the two kinds of syntaxes has interestingly, though, again, roughly, been reworded as a distinction between the syntax of assertion (= what results from the online speaker's choice) and the syntax of presupposition (= what is contextually given).[5]

5 On this topic: Berrendonner (1983), Danon-Boileau & al. (1991). See also Givón (1975) on three Bantu languages.

2

Delimiter particle insertion in Korean and the argument/adjunct ~ disjunct opposition

Let us turn now to an application to an agglutinative language with SOV order: Korean. As mentioned above, tests have been conducted with two particles, called 'delimiters', expressing restriction and addition: particles –*man* 'only' and –*to* 'also'. Both, in contexts where they are licensed, are supposed to indicate a 'paradigmatic slot', so that they are expected to give a basis for the macro-/micro-syntax distinction. However, given that only the first particle has a functional equivalent among the tests proposed for French, it has to be explained why these two particles have been selected, whereas tests relying on cleft formation and negation have been excluded.

G.A.R.S. researchers took over three main tests for stating the macro- or micro-syntactic nature of constituents: pseudo-cleft formation, negation, and restriction. But it should be noted that the three constructions are not mutually incompatible, as illustrated in the following example:

(219) *Ce n'est pas que lui qui est venu.*
"It is not only him/he who came."

Cleft formation has scope over negation which itself has scope over restriction. The order of application can be hierarchically represented as:

CLEFT [NEG [REST [*lui*]]]

In order to preserve the homogeneity of tests (thus, hopefully, the homogeneity of results), it is better to choose constructions that are mutually exclusive, in this case, choose one out of the three possibilities. Cleft formation is excluded in first place because it is much more restricted in Korean than in English or French (see Cho S.Y. (1991), Choi-Jonin I. (2003) for contrastive accounts with respectively English and French). Negation formation is naturally available, but its use as a test can easily be a delicate matter, because negation can receive a metalinguistic interpretation. Also, it can lead to build long and complex test sentences that often sound unnatural.

Eventually there is the use of the restrictive marker. As it can be expressed in many languages as a phonologically light particle, its insertion does not imply much change or unnaturalness in tested sentences. Also, together with the additive marker, with which it is mutually exclusive, it is widely used. In addition, at least in Korean, Japanese, and Mongolian, both particles are less constrained than other particles of the same paradigm. All these properties make tests easier to conduct, and guarantee more homogenous results.

Note that these particles do not always imply paradigmatic variation in the position of the constituent they attach to. Such is the 'idiomatic use' of Kor. addition particle *-to* marking exclamatory utterances, a use that will therefore not be considered as relevant for the tests conducted:

(220) 오늘 밤은 달도 밝구나
*Onul pam.un tal.**to** palk.kuna*
today night.Top clear.TS
"Tonight the moon is so bright!" (vs. "Tonight the moon is bright too")

1. Nominal functions

What is relevant here is to show that the restriction and addition delimiters can attach to regular arguments or argument-like adjuncts with their expected meanings: putting -explicitly or implicitly- the element they attach to in association with other elements of the same paradigm. To ensure that restrictive or additive markers have scope over the tested element only, and not over some larger phrase, it has been inquired whether other elements belonging to the same class can explicitly be added as units contrasting with the first argument. In each case below, informants could interpret the nouns under scope in contrast with other nouns belonging to the same paradigm. This holds for arguments, e.g.: *Myengsik* vs. *Chelswu* (222: e.g. 'Only Myungshik spoke in Korean, Chelswu did not'); *doctor* vs. *nurse* (223); *book* vs. *paper*; *student(s)* vs. *teacher(s)* (224), *I* vs. *other people* (225), as well as for a locative complement, e.g.: *Seoul* vs. *Busan* (226). Example (227) gives an illustration drawn from real data (a song's lyrics) showing a beneficiary complement marked with *–man*: the implicit paradigmatic contrast should not be questionable.

(221)	명식만/도	한국말로	말했다.
	{myengsik}.man/to	*hankwukmal.lo*	*malhay.ss.ta*
	Myungshik.only/also	Korean.Inst	speak.Past.TS

"{Myungshik} spoke in Korean." *vs.* {Chelswu, etc.}

(222)	의사만/도	필요하다.
	{uisa}.man/to	*philyoha.ta*
	doctor.only/also	be_needed.TS

"(I) need {a doctor}." *vs.* {nurse, etc.}

(223)	선생님은	학생에게만/도	책만/도	주었다
	senseyngnim.un	*{hakseyng}.ekey.man/to*	*{chayk}.man/to*	*cwuessta*
	teacher.Top	student.Dest.only/also	book.only/also	gave

"The teacher gave {books} to {the students}." *vs.* {papers, etc.} / {other teachers, etc.}

(224)	나랑만/도	같이	(노래를)	부르자
	{na}.lang.man/to	*kathi*	*(nolay.lul)*	*pwuluca*
	I.with.only/also	together	song.Obj	sing.TS

"Let's sing together {with me}." *vs.* {him, etc.}

(225)

서울에만/도	봄이	왔다
{Sewul.ey}.man/to	*pom.i*	*wassta*
Seoul.only/also	spring.S	came

"Spring came {in Seoul}." *vs.* {Busan, etc.}

(226)

오로지	나를 위해서만	사랑해줄	여자[6]
Oloci	*{na.lul wihayse}.man*	*salanghay.cwu.l*	*yeca.*
solely	I.Obj for.only	love.give.Adn:Fut	woman

"A woman giving her love solely {for me}."

Delimiters here naturally have a narrow scope interpretation, which means that the most natural way of interpreting complements marked by *–to* or *–man* is to draw them out of a set of other possible elements belonging to the same paradigm. Such complements can be said to pertain to the wide government, or to the micro-syntactic part of grammar.

2. Adverbial functions

If a temporal adverb such as *ecey* 'yesterday' behaves as expected in (227) (possible contrast with *onul* 'today'), modal adverbs of the comment type, as in (228) or (229), even if they can occasionally attach the additive marker (228), do not lend their slot open to paradigmatic variation (i.e. the insertion of *–to* is not interpreted as an additive process). There is no possibility to retrieve a set of elements contrasting with *tahaynghi* 'fortunately', or *mullon* 'of course':

(227)

어제만/도	시장에	갔다
{ecey}.man/to	*sicang.ey*	*kassta*
yesterday.only/also	market.Dir	went

"{Yesterday} I've been to the market." *vs.* {today, etc.}

6 (가야랑, 수리수리마수리).

(228)

다행히(도)	뼈는	부러지지 않았다
tahaynghi.(to)	*ppye.nun*	*puleci.ci anhassta*
fortunately.(also)	bone.Top	break.didn't

"Fortunately, he had no broken bones." *vs.* {Ø}

(229) 물론*(도/만)
mullon.(to/man)*
of_course.only/also

"Of course." *vs.* {Ø}

Adverbial clauses may display a different sensitivity to delimiter particles. For instance, the purpose clause in (230) may attach both, with the expected restrictive and additive meanings, but conditional clauses with the suffixes –*myen* or –*ketun*, as well as causal clauses with –*se* or –*nikka* cannot directly attach the particle on their right end. Thus, (18) and (19) are ungrammatical:

(230)

나는	여기에	책을	찾으러	온	거이에요.
{na.nun	*yeki.ey*	*chayk.ul*	*chac.ule}.man/to*	*o.n*	*ke.ieyyo*
I.Top	here.Dir	book.Obj	look_for.for.only/also	come.Adn:Past	thing.Cop

"I went her {to buy a book}." *vs.* {to see you, etc.}

(231)

따뜻해지면,	우리는	공원에	가겠다.
*{ttattushayci.myen}.*man/*to,*	*wuli.nun*	*kongwen.ey*	*kakeyssta*
get_warm.Cond.only/also	we.Top	park.Dir	shall go

"{If it gets warm}, we'll go to the park." *vs.* {Ø}

(232)

제가	집에	없거든	사무실에	전화해주세요.
{cey.ka	*cip.ey*	*eps.ketun}.*man/*to*	*samwusil.ey*	*cenhwahay.cwuseyyo*
I.S	home.Loc	not_be.Cond	office.Loc	call.give

"{If I am not at home}, please call at my office." *vs.* {Ø}

(233)	추워서/추우니까	밖으로	안	나갔어
	*{chwuw.ese/chwuwu. nikka}.*man/*to*	*pakk.ulo*	*an*	*nakasse.*
	cold.Cause/cold.Cause.only/ also	outside.Dir	Neg	went_out

"I didn't go outside {because/since it was cold}." *vs.* {Ø}

In order to get acceptable sentences, one has to attach the delimiters to the root of the main verb in the adverbial clause, then attach the conditional or causal connector to the anaphoric verb *ha-* ('do'). E.g.: *ttattus.man hayci-myen,* [...] "only if it gets warm, [...]".[7]

The peculiarity of such a construction, in contrast with the direct attachment of the suffix to purpose clauses, may indicate that conditional and causal adverbial clauses stand at the border between the syntax of assertion and the syntax of presupposition. It is worth noting that in languages such as English or French, while purpose clauses are always licensed in cleft constructions and acceptable under the scope of restrictive or negative markers, *if*-clauses do not always sound natural in the same contexts (e.g.: ?*It is if you go that I'll go*), while some causal markers never pass the paradigmatic tests (Eng. *since*, Fr. *puisque*).[8]

One step further past the border of assertive syntax, and towards a contextually-bound syntax (i.e. linked with presupposed knowledge), one may find concessive clauses. In Korean, as in Japanese or Mongolian, the additive particle can mark the concessive meaning. There is however no implication of a paradigm. Naturally, it can be argued that there is another element in contrast, that is, the contradictory proposition, for instance "it snowed" *vs.* "it didn't snow", and this may be the explanation why an additive particle appears here, but as contradictory elements, they also cannot coexist in the same paradigmatic set. Moreover, the additive particle can never be substituted for the restrictive one:

7 Example kindly provided by Choi E-jung (Ewha Womans University).

8 Contrast the well-known behavior of *because* vs. (causal) *since* with respect to contrastive focalization through clefting: *It is not {**because** the truth is too difficult to see}* i *that we make mistakes, we make mistakes {**because** the easiest and most comfortable course for us is to seek insight where it accords with our emotions – especially selfish ones}* i. (Alexander Solzhenitsyn) vs. **It is not **since** the truth is too difficult...*

(234) 눈이 와도 집에 있었어요.
*nwun.i wa.to/*man cip.ey issesseyo*
snow.S come.also/only home.Loc stayed
"Also (= even though) {it snowed}, we stayed at home." *vs.* {Ø}

Concessive clauses clearly refer to contents that defy any attempt of explicit paradigmatic variation,[9] and accordingly should be considered as macro-syntactic constituents.

3. Negative proforms

Another striking similarity concerning the additive particles in Korean, Japanese and Mongolian, is their use in forming negative nominal or adverbial proforms. As in the previous case, the insertion of, respectively, *-to*, *-mo* and *ch*, is not interpreted as an additive process:

(235) 아무도 오지 않았다.
*amu.to/*man o.ci anhassta*
誰も 来なかった。
*dare.mo/*dake ko.nakatta*
Хэн ч ирээгүй.
*xen ch/*l iree.güi*

"Nobody came." *vs.* {Ø}

(236) 아무 것도 보이지 않는다.
*amu kes.to/*man poi.ci anhnunta*
何も 見えない。
*nani.mo/*dake mie.nai*
Юу ч үзэхгүй.
*yuu ch/*l üzex.güi*

"(I) can't see anything." *vs.* {Ø}

9 Compare for instance with the behavior of the Eng. concessive marker *although*: **It is although it snowed that we stayed at home*; **We did not stay at home although it snowed, but although we were tired*, etc.

In paradigmatic terms, and this not surprising, there is no conceivable element that could be contrasted to 'nobody' or 'nothing' in the set of persons or the set of things respectively referred to. In addition, there is no possibility to substitute *–to* for *–man*. Negative proforms, together with other proforms (indefinite and interrogative) should be given a very specific status here, whatever their function, given that they occupy micro-syntactic slots without having micro-syntactic properties. They have an outsider status, and so are elements that may serve as tests for the macro-/micro syntax distinction (e.g. the negative, restrictive markers themselves): in the same way, indefinite and interrogative proforms are hints that some parts of grammar allow the construction of paradigmatic sets, even if they are empty.

They also point to the fact that the macro-/micro-syntax distinction made here relies on semantic factors, because they show that knowing the function of a given constituent is not sufficient to determine its macro-/micro-syntactic status. In other words, it is not true that functions such as subjects or objects necessarily have the properties of micro-syntactic constituents. This assumption is important, and more, must be emphasized, insofar as it extends to a great deal of *non pronominal* constituents having regular nominal or adverbial functions, which are even so numerous that one is led to posit not less than another syntactic tier.

3

Fake arguments in compounds and collocations

1. Introduction: Classic diagnostic tests for compounding

If one really tries to apply tests to all possible elements of a sentence, there is not much choice left but to acknowledge that there is another syntactic level below which elements cannot be under the scope of delimiters. This level, which could therefore be named 'nano-syntax', includes constituents below the word level (morphemes) as well as most constituents belonging to noun or prepositional phrases. It can be recalled here that insertion of the Jap. particle *sae* 'even' has been used by Kageyama (1999) for testing the lexical integrity of compounds. In a similar vein, Spencer (2005: 78) notes that "it is generally agreed that displacements which realize information structure, such as topicalization/focussing, scrambling, wh-movement and so on cannot affect parts of words". Here are some Eng. examples quoted in Kageyama (1999: 299):

(237) ?*What do you like (...)ball? > Base(...).*

(238) ?*It is not base(...), but volley(...) that I like (...)balls.*
?*Talking of (...)balls, I only like base(...).*

But Spencer goes on observing that *productively formed* noun-noun "compounds" like *morphology lecture* in *She would never give a morphology lecture* are also "immune from such processes". The list should not end there: many other parts of phrases such as determiners, attributive adjectives, and relative clauses, as well as the head itself, cannot either be *it*-clefted, at least in English (239):

(239) **It is {a} that I met young girl.*
**It is {young} that I met a girl.*
**It is {who was wounded ... } that I met another man.*
**It is {girl} that I met a young.*

Compare now a set of classic criteria for compounding (cleft-formation, topicalization and coordination) applied to *morphology* in *morphology lecture*, which was argued to be a compound, with the same set applied to *young* in *young girl*:

(240) **It is morphology that he gave a lecture.*
**Morphology, he gave a lecture.*
He gave a morphology and syntax lecture.

(241) **It is young that I met a girl.*
**Young, I met a girl.*
I met a young and pretty girl.

What these and other syntactic tests may tell us is simply that elements such as constituents of noun phrases behave in a similar way with respect to some syntactic rules, but they are by no way conclusive on the lexicon/syntax distinction. To make this point clearer, let us take an example of another Adj + N sequence, say *green house*. In one interpretation, it depicts a house that is green (syntactic formation, with a compositional meaning), while in another, it refers to a building designed for growing plants, in which case, the sequence is seen as a lexical formation. But from *I have seen a green house*, neither topicalization nor clefting can be used to distinguish one structure from the other, because they give the same negative results whatever the intended interpretation is:

(242) **It's green that I have seen a house.*
**Green, I have seen a house.*

Wh-question formation, on the other hand, is licensed only for the syntactic formation, since *green house* as a compound is not a 'sort of house':

(243) – *Which/what kind of house did you see?*
– *The green one/A green house.*

How should then (the) *White House* be classified? It is indeed a sort of house, and question formation is allowed as above. Yet it has a specific status: even though its meaning (casually?) happens to be componential, the combination displays frozen morphosyntactic properties. For instance, the article is always definite, the adjective cannot be modified by an adverb (**The very/poorly/... White House*) or serve in the predicative function (**The House is white*). In addition, it can be considered as a proper noun designating only one entity in the extra-linguistic world, and said to belong to the class of 'animate locations' due to its specific selection properties (cf. *I visited the White House*, *The White House decided that...*, *According to the White House*).

It should be clear then that most syntactic tests used as criteria for compounding do not distinguish lexical units from 'syntactically formed units' such as complex noun phrases. Naturally, these tests that also serve for the macro-/micro-syntax distinction cannot either be interpreted in terms of syntax vs. lexicon. In the present case as well, it makes more sense to speak of another sort of syntax, namely a 'nano-syntax'. This syntactic level below 'regular syntax' will be illustrated further in collocational sentences.

2. Fake arguments in collocational sequences

It will be shown here that some constituents (i) that cannot be considered as parts of compounds, and (ii) that can be marked as regular verb arguments –whatever their function– do not actually behave as regular arguments. Specifically, even though they can attach a delimiter, their actual scope is not solely the noun phrase, but the whole [noun+verb] complex. Thus, when asked to retrieve elements in contrast, informants cannot give contrasting nouns, and rather give contrasting complexes, with a different noun and a different verb (this option is possible also with regular arguments). The sharp sign (#) in examples (245-249) indicates when the most likely interpretation of the sentence involves a wide scope contrast. Let look first at expressions involving a subject.

In (244), the restrictive particle *–man* was rejected by my first informant on the subject of the expression 'eye-got_far = be blind'. Choi E-J. (pers. comm.) found it however fine in opposition with e.g. 'be healthy', 'be great', etc. *–To* 'also' is licensed with the subject 'eyes' only if the whole sequence is interpretated metaphorically as 'lose one's reason', and thus can stand in paradigmatic contrast with other misdeeds (*topak.to heyssta* 'gambled', *mayak.to hayssta* 'took drugs', etc.). (245) and (246) accept both the restrictive and additive particles on the subjects belly and throat, and typically stand in contrast with each other ("I am only hungry, I am not thirsty"), and there is no contrasting subject available for a same predicate, in other words nothing else than (somebody's) belly that could be hungry, or than (somebody's) throat that could be dry. The subject *palam* 'wind' in (247), 'wind is blowing' can have *–man* attached. The sentence, not so natural for my informant, could however be uttered as a reply to someone worrying about a sound, and it would be understood with a wide scope interpretation ("It's only wind that is blowing").[10] *–to* instead of *–man* would also get a wide scope and mean "And on top of this, it's also windy" (not only does it rain...).

Finally, the example in (248) is one of the most micro-syntactic-like sequence, in that its subject can contrast with other potential strong characteristics, although it most naturally goes along with other collocations, such as 'be smart'.

10 Choi E-jung (pers. comm.) judges it however natural in various contexts. An anonymous reviewer also agreed that all examples from (244) to (248) were all fine with a large scope.

(244)	X	눈*만/#도	멀었다.
		*nwun.*man/#to*	*melessta*
		eye.only/also	got_far

"X is blind." *vs.* {??}

(245)	X	배#만/#도	고프다.
		pay.#man/#to	*kophuta*
		belly.only/also	hungry

"X is hungry." *vs.* {be thirsty, tired, etc.}

(246)	X	목#만/#도	마르다.
		mok.#man/#to	*maluta*
		throat.only/also	dry

"X is thirsty." *vs.* {be hungry, etc.}

(247)	바람#만/#도	불고 있다.
	palam.#man/#to	*pwul.ko_issta*
	wind.only/also	blow.Prog

"Wind is blowing." *vs.* {??}

(248)	X	힘(#)만/(#)도	세다.
		him.(#)man/(#)to	*seyta*
		energy.only/also	strong

"X is strong." *vs.* {be smart}

Similar answers were obtained in:

(249): an object like 'tobacco' in 'smoke tobacco' (e.g., with –*man*: X does nothing else than smoking (tobacco is implied); with -*to*: exclamation or contrast with 'drink alcohol');

(250): the locative complement 'outside' in 'go outside' (–*man* is strange, since there is no other choice than going outside, but possible if meaning "I did nothing else (e.g. I didn't hit him) than going outside"; –*to* would be acceptable in the context "I looked for it inside and I also went outside");

(251): the object 'study' of the support verb construction 'do study' (e.g., contrast with 'watch TV, play games, etc.').

(249) X 담배#만/#도 피운다.
tambay.#man/#to *phiwunta*
tobacco.only/also smoke
"X smokes tobacco." *vs.* {drink alcohol, etc.}

(250) 밖으로#만/#도 나갔다.
pakkuro.#man/#to *nakassta*
outside.only/also went_out
"I went outside." *vs.* {look for something inside}

(251) 공부#만/#도 해라.
kongpwu.#man/#to *hay.la.*
study.only/also do
"Study!" *vs.* {watch TV, play games, etc.}

3. The syllepsis principle

1) Semantic clashes and paradigmatic weirdness

Even though the nominal constituents of the sentences above display the functions and marks of regular arguments, they do not behave like micro-syntactic constituents, because they are not in a slot where paradigmatic variation is allowed. Even if they attach delimiters, these have (or, in some cases, tend more naturally to have) a wide scope interpretation: the only possible contrast holds with other verb complexes or collocational sequences. Indeed, any attempt to put another argument in contrast would led to a case of semantic incongruity close to what is otherwise known as a figure of speech, namely a **syllepsis**. Examples of syllepsis, as in (252-253), show that the sole fact that a given verb accepts various complements does not imply that they belong to the same set. The cause for the semantic clash observed in these examples is not of syntactic nature, but is due to a paradigmatic weirdness. The reason for the awkwardness of coordination in (252) and (253) is the same as that of contrast in the previously presented test sentences.

(252) *Mr Jones took his coat and his leave.* → *take {coat, leave}
You held your breath and the door for me. → *hold {breath, door}

(253) *Après avoir sauté sa belle-sœur et le repas du midi,* → *sauter (belle-sœur, repas)
le Petit Prince reprit enfin ses esprits et une banane. → *reprendre (esprits, banane)
(Pierre Desproges)
"After having 'jumped' his sister-in law (= fucked) and the lunch (= skipped),
the Little Prince 'took again' his spirits (= recovered) and a banana (= took another)."

A generalized 'syllepsis principle' could be called upon here that would account for the ungrammaticality or unnaturalness of sequences where the governing word is somehow forced to accept paradigmatic variation in a complement slot that does not constitute a proper set.

The process at work here is very close to what Halliday (1967), speaking of cognate objects, termed a 'mutual expectancy of collocation between the noun and the verb involved':

> Cognateness is best thought of as 'extension inherent in the process' leading to a mutual expectancy of collocation between the noun and the verb involved. (Halliday, 1967: 59)

As a matter of fact, cognate object constructions only accept a wide scope contrast when they attach a delimiter.[11] Let us give here another attested utterance in Korean:

11 All things being equal, that is when they do not have an attributive extension, in which case the scope may be narrower thanks to the attribute: e.g. *dream only bad dreams. / live only one's life*. Such constructions recover their expected micro-syntactic properties (see also focalization, question formation, etc.) and have to be differentiated from cognate object constructions where the object is normally not otherwise expanded (cf. Kor. *kkwum kkwuta* 'dream', *chwum chwuta* 'dance'). Cognate object constructions seem to play very different roles in European and Asian languages.

(254) 밤늦게까지 먹고 마시면서 ... (kids.hankooki.com/lpage/)
Pam.nuckey.kkaci mek.ko masi.myense ...
night.late.until eat.and drink.while ...

... 노래도 부르고 춤도 췄습니다.
... nolay.to pwulu.ko ***chwum.to chw****.ess.supnita*
... song.also sing.and **dance.also danse**.PAST.ST

"Until late at night, while eating and drinking, we sang songs and danced (danses)."

In (254), no noun other than the cognate object *chwum* 'dance' can be retrieved as a potential additive object of *chwuta* 'to dance', despite the presence of the delimiter *–to* 'also'. There is indeed an additive meaning, but bearing on the whole cognate object construction, that is 'dance dances' in addition to 'sing songs'.

There is no doubt that numerous verb-argument constructions would fall under the 'syllepsis principle', and among them one should expect many support verb constructions, synthetic compounds or pseudo compounds, cognate object constructions, and even meteorological clauses. Korean facts presented here should not be surprising since it would not be difficult to find similar phenomena in European languages, and test again the licensing of paradigmatic variation.

(255) *Bill kicked the bucket.*
→ **It is the bucket that Bill kicked.*
→ **Bill kicked the bucket only, not ...*
→ **Bill did not kick the bucket, he kicked ...*
(see also question formation: **What did Bill kick?*)

2) Metaphor and syllepsis: *On ne voit bien qu'avec le cœur, l'essentiel est invisible pour les yeux*

The two figures of speech *metaphor* and *syllepsis* entertain a privileged relationship.

Idiomatic formations such as 'kick the bucket' most naturally fall under the syllepsis principle: since the semantic interpretation cannot be inferred from the individual components (i.e. taken in isolation), but rather construed at the level of their combination, any attempt to individuate one of the elements inside a paradigm *of its own* is doomed to failure. The metaphoric interpretation does not survive outside of its domain of application. This holds on the syntagmatic as well as on the paradigmatic axis. Let us assume for instance that 'bucket' metaphorically stands for 'life', or at least, that it is linked to somebody's existence. Such an interpretation cannot emerge from another combination such as **risk the bucket* (for 'risk one's life'), and does not apply to any other entity that could very naturally be related to 'bucket', e.g. a spade: in *He kicked the bucket and the spade*, there is no metaphoric rule telling us to interpret 'spade' as somehow related to somebody's existence. In other terms, the metaphoric interpretation cancels previously existing syntagmatic and paradigmatic relationships.

Even in the case of 'conceptual metaphors' (Lakoff), understood as a general pattern following which metaphors are regularly associated with a given domain, e.g. love conceived as war, it is not the case that all concepts syntagmatically or paradigmatically linked to the desired output have a corresponding element in the input domain, and conversely. If love is a conquest, it does not imply that lovers are soldiers: we can understand the metaphor in *She was besieged by suitors*, not in *She was besieged by soldiers* (not to speak of 'ennemies'...).

Now perfectly transparent combinations such as 'belly-hungry' also fall under the syllepsis principle. This was implicitly explained by the fact that no other entity than the belly can be conceivably related to 'be hungry'. The fact that the body-part involved is unique in the paradigm selected by the predicate does actually not depend that much on referential grounds than on linguistic constraints. First, the conception that a belly rather than its possessor can be hungry is a language-specific constraint, that is not allowed in all languages. Second, it is easy to imagine that other body parts could be hungry as well, like one's heart (for love) or one's brain (for ideas). This would again depend on the set of conceptualizations available in a specific language, but nevertheless imply a possibility of paradigmatic variation in the subject slot. Yet trials to play on this variation may also lead to semantic incongruity, because the contrasted elements themselves may have to be metaphorically interpreted. Consequently, sequences such as *Only his belly is hungry, not his heart* may be rejected by informants for the same reason as illustrated above for idiomatic expressions.

This is only a theoretical example, and the acceptability of such or such sequence should not be presupposed before it is tested. Let us take another example and illustrate a bit of the complexity of the phenomenon. When the expression 'age-young' in Mongolian was tested, my informant found it perfectly acceptable in contrast with 'idea/mind-young' (i.e. "Only his age is young, not his ideas"). Here, one cannot decide whether the combination of ideas with young is a metaphor or not before knowing if the term for young is restricted to animate entities. Such observations just amount to emphasizing the importance of testing.

4

Towards a three-leveled syntax

Specialists of compounds and collocations know and have been using tests for a long time, but mostly for proving frozeness in the *syntagmatic cohesiveness* (stated in terms of (in)separability) of this or that sequence. It should be emphasized here (i) that neither compounds nor collocations are exceptional in their resistance to paradigmatic variation (i.e. they are not singled out from many other kinds of word combinations); (ii) that sequences that are syntactically well-formed and semantically transparent (such as the redundant SPC mentioned under 3.3.2), p. 194sq sq.) may also prove resistant to paradigmatic variation. In addition to their obvious cross-linguistic applicability, with respect to collocations as well as to other elements, these tests are expected to provide a useful, reliable, and typologically friendly means of classification of elements in a sentence.

For the sake of comparison, some of the data that were elicited from Mongolian, a language that shares many structural features with Korean, will be added. It aims to point out some differences in the use of delimiters[12] but can also lead to the conclusion that the results match to a significant extent for what regards the micro-syntax vs. nano-

12 The most commonly used restriction and addition markers are respectively Kor. *-man* (만), Mong. *-l* (л), and Kor. *-to* (도), Mong. *-ch* (ч). They are to be considered as clitics, attached at the end of words (but they are written as separate words Mongolian). Quite often, they are used together with lexemes having the same meaning, as Kor. *yoksi* and Mong. *bas*, both meaning 'also'. It is irrelevant here whether, and in which order, they may combine or not with case particles (in Mongolian, delimiters always follow case markers). See Kang S. (2004) for a contrastive account.

syntax distinction. The detailed answers provided by my informants[13] cannot be reproduced here, so that the chart displays only the main information, that is whether the delimiter is licensed on the constituent in curly brackets, and with what scope interpretation when explicitly put in contrast: narrow scope, i.e. on the constituent only ('+'), or wide scope ('wide'). A 'Ø' indicates that the answer was not available because of structural particulars of the language investigated, e.g. the absence of a given structure):

	Korean		Mongolian	
	만 *-man*	도 *-to*	л *-l*	ч *-ch*
Subjects {M.} spoke in English	+	+	+	+
(To) me {doctor} is_needed 'I need a doctor'	+	+	+	+
(To) me {two books} exist 'I have two books'	+	+	Ø	Ø
{Wind} is blowing	wide	wide	wide/+	wide
{Rain} came/fell/entered 'It rained'	wide	wide	–/wide	wide/+
X {strength} strong 'X is strong'	wide/+	wide/+	Ø	Ø
X {age} young 'X is young'	+	?+	+	+
X {throat/mouth} dry/thirsty 'X is thirsty'	wide	wide	wide	wide
X {belly} hungry/empty 'X is hungry'	wide	wide	wide	wide
X {eye} blind 'X is blind'	–	wide	?wide	wide
Other functions *Accusative:* Did you see {this movie}?	+	+	+	(–) [бас]
X gave {books} to the students	+	+	+	+
Do {study}! 'Study!'	wide	wide	wide	wide
X smokes {tobacco}	wide	wide	wide	wide

13 The data were collected thanks to Lee Jaymin (Korean) and Turtogtoh Janar (Mongolian), both good informants and good friends.

Dative: X gave books {to the students}	+	+	+	+
I went {outside}	(wide)	wide	wide	wide
Allative: I want to go {to Mongolia}	+	+	+	+
Comitative: Sing {with me}	+	+	+	+
Instrumental: X spoke {in English}	+	+	+	+
Location: Spring came {in London}	+	+	(+)	+
Comparative: T. is taller {than M.}	+	(+)	+	+
Temporal/aspectual adverbs {Yesterday} I went to the market	+	+	+	+
{Sometimes} I go to the market.	–	–	(same meaning)	(wide)
Nominalized clause A book hard {to understand}	+	wide/ (+)	+	+
Purpose I went here {to take books} Kor. *–le* Mong. *–хаар*	 + Ø	 + Ø	 Ø +	 Ø +
Cause				
Kor. *–se / –nikka*	(+)	(+)	Ø	Ø
Mong. *–хоор / учраас*	Ø	Ø	+	(+)
Conditional {If (the weather) gets warm}, [...].				
Kor. *–myen / –ketun*	(+)	(+)	Ø	Ø
Mong. *–бол*	Ø	Ø	+	(+)
Concessive Also (= 'even if') {it snowed}, I stayed at home.	–	Ø	–	Ø

As can be seen from the chart, the overlap of identical answers for structurally similar constructions is striking. Yet, if the optionality of arguments involved in some collocations were to be taken into account, the overall picture would be quite different. For instance, the subjects 'belly' and 'throat' in Korean expressions for respectively 'being hungry' and 'being thirsty' (lit. 'belly-hungry' and 'throat-dry') are rarely omitted, therefore are not normally optional, while they are in Mongolian. If one were consistent with the criterium of optionality, one would consider that 'belly' or 'throat' in the respective collocational sequences are arguments in Korean but adjuncts in Mongolian. Moreover, emphasis on the non-optionality would lead to the conclusion that in Korean, 'arguments' involved in collocational sequences are more argument-like than 'arguments' in free sequences, because the former are usually optional whereas the latter are not. Usually, when one has to say that he is hungry in Korean, there is no need to express the first person; the order and optionality of the constituents in such a sentence could be pictured as follows:

(256) (I.Top/S) belly.(S) hungry.

Using here the labels 'adjunct' for the first –optional– subject, and 'argument' for the second –(quasi) obligatory– subject, would be, from the point of view developped here, quite misleading. As a matter of fact, it would fail to recognize the collocational nature of the relation between Subj2 and the predicate, as opposed to the free combinatorial nature of Subj1. In other terms, fail to pinpoint the domain where the speaker has a real choice in combining units, which is beyond doubt what underlies our implicit conception of what syntax is designed for.

Now, units belonging to 'nano-syntax' can still be described as displaying some sort of syntax, not only because their apparent output is often very similar to that of micro-syntax, but also because there are (i) placement rules and (ii) selection restrictions (as in morphology proper).

The same claim can be made for discourse elements, although a thorough investigation of their placement rules and, above all, of their selection restrictions, remains to be undertaken.[14]

I therefore advocate for the existence of a three-leveled syntax in which the three main typical domains of application would be: (1) the

---

14 For instance, it has been noted that interaction adverbs may be restricted to some sentence types and excluded from others. See for instance *frankly* in **Frankly, come with me.*

'core syntax' with the verb and its arguments and argument-like adjuncts, (2) the syntax of various discourse and context-bound elements, (3) the syntax of collocational sequences and compounds (possibly covering morphology as well):

A three-leveled syntax:

	Disjunct syntax = 'macro-syntax'	**Core syntax = 'micro-syntax'**	**Collocational syntax = 'nano-syntax'**
Typical domain of application	Modal disjuncts Comment disjuncts	**Verb + (free) arguments** **Verb + (free) adjuncts**	Compounds Collocations

As a final remark, in opposition to micro-syntactic constituents, discourse elements and elements of collocations have the same property of not being able to be explicitly or implicitly contrasted. Why is that so? Does this mean that they share a common feature? The main reason, as the tests used, is certainly to be formulated in negative terms: they do not belong to the assertive part of the utterance. Discourse elements, as already mentioned, are linked to contextual presupposed knowledge, whereas elements of set expressions, not to speak of the internal components of words, most certainly belong to a common mental lexicon (in a wide sense, because it can also involve combinations of words) shared by the speakers of a given community. So that, when a speaker takes its turn, the informational content implied by those elements is already decided.

Conclusion

நாம் அவன் இவன் உவன்	nām avan ivan uvan
அவள் இவள் உவள் எவள்	aval ival uval eval
தாம் அவர் இவர் உவர்	tām avar ivar uvar
அது இது உது எது	atu itu utu etu
வீம்அவை இவைஉவை	vīm avai ivai uvai
அவை நலம் தீங்கவை	avai nalam tīnku avai
ஆம்அவை ஆயவை அய்	ām avai āy avai
நின்ற அவரே.	āy ninra avarē

We here and that man, this man,
and that other in-between,
and that woman, this woman,
and that over, whoever,

those people, and these,
and these others in-between,
this thing, that thing,
and this other in-between, whichever,

all things dying, these things,
those things, those other in-between,
good things, bad things,
things that were, that will be,

being all of them,
he stands there.
(Nammālvār, *The Paradigm*[1])

This study thoroughly investigated the properties of frozen sequences, usual in Korean as in many other Asian languages, involving the combination of a subject nominal and a predicate. It has been shown that most such instances cannot be considered as compounds, even though they doubtlessly show lexicalization effects.

Several notions and tests that were discussed here belong to the traditional set of tools that linguists commonly use in the description of structurally diverse languages. They were by no means rejected, but it was necessary to adapt and/or make more precise their domain of application. In languages in which the border between the syntax of free combinations and that of frozen combination is blurried by many factors (such as the absence –cf. isolating languages– or, conversely the presence – cf. agglutinative languages– of regular grammatical material in both areas), the *syntagmatic* frozenness of verb phrases cannot be assessed in the same way as in European languages.

When considering Korean SPC, a purely syntagmatic approach often proved to be either irrelevant, or to give counter-intuitive results. Let us remind the reader of two such unwishable results:

A few occurrences of subject-predicate sequences were observed with the preverbal negation *an-* occurring before the nominal: as this does not happen with, for instance, longer adjectival verbs, SPC could be considered as 'better words' than simple words (cf. Ch. 2).

Korean subjects in collocations strongly tend to be obligatory, whereas subjects in free sequences are normally optional: subject nouns in SPC could therefore be considered as 'better subjects' than regular subjects (cf. Ch. 3).

These observations are representative of many contradictory properties of SPC that were noted throughout this study, for Korean as well as for other Asian languages (cf. Ch. 1): subject-predicate collocations can display both a high degree of lexicalization and a high degree of morphosyntactic freedom. As was strongly advocated for in the second chapter, this implies that lexicalization effects, or 'wordhood'

1 In: A. K. Ramanujan, trans., *Hymns for the drowning: Poems for Vishnu*, Penguin Books, 2005, p. 122.

in a wide sense, is largely disconnected from syntagmatic frozenness, which refers here to the cohesion (i.e. inseparability, fusion, etc.) of segments on the phonological as well as on the morphosyntactic level. To which can be added the unfaithful criterion of semantic frozenness (i.e. non-componentiality of meaning).

The perspective of paradigmatic frozenness, as tested with the help of additive and restrictive markers, had on the other hand given positive and distinctive results on the sequences considered here. It allowed a similar analysis and grouping of collocations and compounds but also of components below the word level (see the notion 'nano-syntax' as developped in Ch. 3). This is a wishable result for the lexicographic description of Korean. It also proved able to deal with semantically perfectly transparent collocations of the redundant type (e.g. 'belly-hungry', 'strength-strong', etc.), that are also observed in South Asian languages, and this gives ground for a study of areal convergences in SPC throughout the Eastern part of Eurasia.

Such an areal study would no doubt cast an interesting light on referential strategies and their correlates in different types of languages.

As a matter of fact, the extension of redundant SPC roughly coincides with the area of numeral classifiers: languages in Southeast Asia as well as Chinese, Korean, and Japanese display systems of numeral classifiers as well as redundant SPC. An attempt could be made to explain this copresence in terms of "referential strategy routines", whereby something is predicated of an entity with or without the medium of an other entity related to the latter.[2]

According to Fauconnier (1985), "if two objects A and B are linked by some pragmatic function, a description of A may be used to identify B", so that we can understand the proper noun *Plato* as referring to *Plato's books* in the sentence *I read Plato*. This kind of indirect reference is so pervasive in daily communication that one could argue it is a matter of pragmatics (the way speakers use natural languages) rather than a matter of linguistics proper. In addition, it is not always possible

2 Concerning the semantic issue of "direct vs. indirect reference", see Borkin (1972), Fauconnier (1985), Langacker (1984, 1987), and a critical review in Kleiber (1991).

to uncover the supposedly intended referential target. Compare for instance sentences (a-d) to (e-f):

(a) **Fred** (= Fred's body) weighs 200 pounds. (Wierzbicka 1976)
(b) She heard the **piano** (= the sound of the piano). (Langacker 1984)
(c) **I** (= my name)'m in the phone book. (Langacker 1984)
(d) **Paul** (*vs.* Paul's skin) is tanned. (Kleiber 1991)
(e) Your dog bit my **cat** (= ??my cat's flesh/cat's skin). (Langacker 1984)
(f) **Fred** (= ??Fred's person/Fred's soul) loves Claire. (Wierzbicka 1976)

Kleiber (1991) convincingly argues that sentences such as *Paul is tanned* do not mean the same as *Paul's skin is tanned*, and shows consequently that in the non-mediated referential strategy illustrated in *Paul is tanned*, there is no need to recover a hidden entity such as *skin*. In other terms, he claims that *Paul* refers to "Paul" and not to "Paul's skin". Nevertheless, languages may differ in using more or less the "indirect reference" strategy to describe specific states of affairs. In Korean, for example, as reported in Na Y-H (1986: 167), a literal translation of *Harry is big* does not sound very natural. A more natural translation has to specify that it is precisely Harry's size or body that is "big", literally "(As for) Harry, body size (is) big":

(257) *Harry.nun momcip.i khuta*
Harry.Top body-size.Subj big
"Harry is big."

Even though the sequence *momcip.i khuta* "body size.Subj (be) big" is rather free in terms of paradigmatic variation allowed in the subject slot, a great wealth of SPC in Korean and in other Asian languages illustrate the same explicit, mediated, referential strategy, because the usual pattern involves a metonymical relationship. Other examples include:

Chinese	口渴 年迈	*kǒukě* *niánmài*	(mouth-thirsty) (age-advanced in years)	"thirsty" "old, aged, senile"
Naxi	—	*nvlmei ga*	(heart good)	"kind&morally good"
Japanese	幅広い 気恥かしい	*haba-biroi* *ki-azukashii*	(width-wide) (spirit-shameful)	"wide, broad" "ashamed"
Korean	배고프다 값싸다	*pay-kophuta* *kaps-ssata*	(belly-hungry) (price-cheap)	"hungry" "cheap"
Kambera	kendar eti nggauru eti	— —	(humble liver) (glad liver)	"humble, meek" "glad"
Vietnamese	hả dạ sáng dạ	— —	(content stomach) (intelligent belly)	"content, satisfied" "intelligent"
Thai	แข็ง-แรง หู-หนวก เบิกบาน-ใจ	*khɛŋ rɛɛŋ* *hŭu nùak* *bəəkbaan cay*	(strength-strong) (ear-deaf) (happy-heart)	"strong" "deaf" "cheerful"

This mediated strategy routine may be shared at different degrees by other languages, but it is undoubtly particularly pervasive in Asian-type languages, where its use seems to parallel that of numeral classifiers. To be sure, one can consider that the use of classifiers for counting entities that are perceptually salient as individuals, such as (Japanese) dogs in (258),[3] is, from a European point of vew, quite redundant:

(258) 犬三匹
inu san-biki
dog three-CL:animal
"three dogs"

3 Some authors seem to claim that users of classifiers conceptualize all entities as non-discrete entities, so that Jap. *inu* here does not mean "dog", but something like "dogness". If true, it is nevertheless safe to assume that such a linguistic conceptualization has not much bearing on everyday behaviour: Japanese people are not particularly inclined to pour buckets with dogs.

Although in this case, the predication (i.e. numeration) is not mediated through a part-whole relationship, but through a –usually– member-class relationship (dog < animal), the process is essentially the same as in Subject-Predicate Collocations of the type seen above. It is again a mediated referential strategy.

Now one should keep in mind that this strategy may be used in European-type languages as well. Precisely, whenever the property which is being predicated does not show a strong and salient correlation with the entity talked about. Such is numeration with mass nouns: there is no reason why *two water(s)* should mean "two liters of water" or "two glasses of water". Here one is compelled to make use of a subtype of classifiers, namely quantifiers. In the same vein, we cannot infer from *Harry is long* that it is his legs, his neck, or his thumb that are/is long, so that the mediated strategy is of the unavoidable kind. For putatively cognitive reasons, *two bottles of water* or *Harry's legs are long* do not seem as redundant as (*Eng) *two people of workers* or (?Eng) *Harry's heart is happy.*

The following chart is likely to idealize the opposition between European-type languages and Asian-type languages, in terms of tendencial constraints related to the use of the mediated strategy when referring to physical descriptions (1-2) and numeration (3-4):

	Physical descriptions	**European-type languages**	**Asian-type languages**
(1a)	*Harry is tall.*	+	–
(1b)	*Harry's size is tall.*	–	+
(2a)	**Harry is long.* (when referring to Harry's legs)	–	–
(2b)	*Harry's legs are long /* *Harry is long-legged.*	+	+
	Numeration		
(3a)	*Two pencils*	+	–

(3b)	*Two "long-objects" of pencil*	–	+
(4a)	**Two waters* (when referring to a quantity of water)	–	–
(4b)	*Two bottles of water*	+	+

It aims however at linking the description of singular phenomena such as those described in this study to an old-fashioned and yet still desirable aim of the *science of languages*, namely knowing a little bit more about how we speak of the world.

References

Adelman, Allison. 2002. *On the status of N-V verbal compounds in Catalan*. Thesis, Swarthmore.

Andréasson, Daniel. 2001. *Active languages*. B.A., Stockholm University.

Arnaud, Pierre J. L. 2003. Les composés timbre-poste. Lyon: Presses universitaires de Lyon.

Aarts, Bas. 2001. *English syntax and argumentation*. New York: Palgrave Macmillan.

Barbaud, P. E. 1994. Conversion syntaxique. *Linguisticæ Investigationes* 18. 1-26.

Bárdosi, Vilmos. 1989. Un ange passe: Contribution à l'étymologie d'une locution. In: Gréciano, Gertrud, ed. *Europhras 88. Phraséologie contrastive*. Strasbourg: Université des sciences humaines. 7-16.

Berrendonner, Alain. 1983. Connecteurs pragmatiques et anaphore. *Cahiers de linguistique française* 5. 215-246.

Berrendonner, Alain. 1991. Pour une macro-syntaxe. In: Willems, Dominique, ed. *Données orales et théories linguistiques*. Paris/Louvain: Duculot. 25-31.

Beyer, Stephan V. 1992. *The Classical Tibetan language*. Albany: State University of New York Press.

Bierbach, M. 1983. Les composés de type *portefeuille*: Essai d'analyse historique. *Travaux de Linguistique et de Littérature* 1983/1. 137-155.

Bisetto, Antonietta. 1999. Note sui composti VN dell'italiano. In: Benincà, Paola & al., eds. *Fonologia e morfologia dell'italiano e dei dialetti d'Italia. Atti del XXXI Congresso SLI.* Roma: Bulzoni editore. 555-589.

Blanche-Benveniste, Claire & al. 1990. *Le français parlé: Études grammaticales*. Paris: C.N.R.S.

Blanche-Benveniste, Claire. 2002. Macro-syntaxe et micro-syntaxe: les dispositifs de la rection verbale. In: Andersen, A. L. & Nølke, H., eds. *Macro-syntaxe et macro-sémantique*. Berne: Peter Lang. 95-118.

Bork, Hans Dieter. 1990. *Die lateinisch-romanischen Zusammensetzungen Nomen + Verb und der Ursprung der romanischen Verb-Ergänzung-Komposita*. Bonn: Romanistischer Verlag.

Borkin, Ann. 1972. Coreference and beheaded NP's. *Papers in Linguistics* 5. 28-45.

Bossong, Georg. 1985. *Empirische Universalienforschung: Differentielle Objektmarkierung in den neuiranischen Sprachen*. Tübingen: Gunter Narr.

Bresnan, Joan. 2001. *Lexical-functional syntax*. Oxford: Blackwell.

Burger, Harald; Buhofer, Annelies & Sialm, Ambros, eds. 1982. *Handbuch der Phraseologie*. Berlin: Walter de Gruyter.

Chappell, Hilary M. 1996. Inalienability and the personal domain in Mandarin Chinese discourse. In: Chappell, H. & McGregor, W., eds. *The grammar of inalienability*. 465-527.

Chen, Chung-Yu. 1984. Neutral tone in Mandarin: Phonotactic description and the issue of the norm. *Journal of Chinese Linguistics* 12:2. 299-333.

Cheng, Chin-chuan. 1973. *A synchronic phonology of Mandarin Chinese*. The Hague: Mouton.

Cheon, Mi-Ae. 2007. Korean phraseology. In: Burger, Harald & al., eds. *Phraseologie/ Phraseology. An international handbook of contemporary research*, Vol. 2. Berlin: Walter de Gruyter. 766-778.

Chi, Telee R. 1985. *A lexical analysis of verb-noun compounds in Mandarin Chinese*. Taipei: The Crane Publishing Co.

Cho, Hang-B[em]. 1992. *Tasi ssun wuli mal ewen iyaki* [Stories of Korean etymology revisited]. Seoul: Hanguk Munwon.

Cho, See-Young. 1991. *Focusing in English and Korean*. Frankfurt: Lang.

Cho, Young-mee Yu. 1994. Verbal compounds in Korean. In: Kim-Renaud, Young-Key, ed. *Theoretical issues in Korean linguistics*. Stanford: CSLI. 29-44.

Choi-Jonin, Injoo. 2003. A propos de focalisation d'un constituant en français et en coréen. In: Herslund, Michael, dir. *Aspects linguistiques de la traduction*. Presses Universitaires de Bordeaux. 125-147.

Choi-Jonin, Injoo; Park, Ok-Hee & You, Jong-Suk. 1994. Les prédicatifs en coréen. *Scolia* 2. 13-53.

Clark, Marybeth. 1996. Where do you feel? Stative verbs and body-part terms in Mainland Southeast Asia. In: Chappell, H. & McGregor, W., eds. 529-564.

Danon-Boileau, Laurent; Morel, Mary-Annick & Meunier, André. 1991. Intégration discursive et intégration syntaxique. *Langages* 104. 111-128.

Dardano, Maurizio. 1978. *La formazione delle parole nell'italiano di oggi*. Roma.

Darmesteter, Arsène. 1894. *Traité de la formation des mots composés dans la langue française comparée aux autres langues romanes et au latin*. Paris: Honoré Champion.

Deulofeu, Henri-José. 2007. Écritures anciennes, paroles actuelles: la grammaire et structures discursives dans les textes médiévaux et dans l'oral contemporain. Ms (Zürich, Romanisches Seminar).

Dixon, Robert Malcom Ward. 1994. *Ergativity*. Cambridge: Cambridge University Press.

Do-Hurinville, Danh Thanh. 2007. Les verbes de qualité en vietnamien. *Travaux linguistiques du Cerlico* 20. 217-233.

Do-Hurinville, Danh Thanh. 2013. De la copule au focalisateur *là* en vietnamien: Bref regard typologique. *Faits de Langues* 41. 41-54.

Donohue, Mark. 2004. Typology and linguistic areas. *Oceanic Linguistics* 43/1. 221-239.

Durie, Mark. 1987. Grammatical relations in Acehnese. *Studies in Language* 11:2. 365-399.

Enfield, Nicholas James. 2003. *Linguistics epidemiology: semantics and grammar of language contact in mainland Southeast Asia*. London: Routledge.

Fauconnier, Gilles. 1985. *Mental spaces*. Cambridge: MIT Press.

Fukushima, Kazuhiko. 1992. Phrase structure grammar, Montague semantics, and floating quantifiers in Japanese. *Linguistics & Philosophy* 14. 581-628.

Gather, Andreas. 2001. *Romanische Verb-Nomen-Komposita. Wortbildung zwischen Lexikon, Morphologie und Syntax*. Tübingen: Gunter Narr.

Giurescu, Anca. 1975. *Les mots composés dans les langues romanes*. The Hague/Paris.

Givón, Talmy. 1975. Focus and the scope of assertion: some Bantu evidence. *Studies in African Linguistics* 6. 185-205.

Goddard, Cliff. 2005. *The languages of East and Southeast Asia*. Oxford: Oxford University Press.

Greenbaum, Sidney & Quirk, Randolph. 1990. *A student's grammar of the English language*. Harlow: Longman.

Guntsetseg, Dolgor. 2009. Differential object marking in (Khalkha)-Mongolian. In: Shibagaki, R. & Vermeulen, R., eds. *MIT Working Papers in Linguistics (MWPL) 58, Proceedings of the 5th Workshop on Formal Altaic Linguistics (WAFL 5)*. 115-129.

Ha, Chi-Kun. 2002. *Hyenday wuri malpon* [A modern grammar]. Pak-i-ceng.

Halliday, Michael Alexander Kirkwood. 1967. Notes on transitivity and theme in English (Pt. 1). *Journal of Linguistics* 3:1. 37-81.

Hashimoto, Mantaro J., ed. 1976. *Genetic relationship, diffusion, and typological aimilarities of East and Southeast Asian languages*. Tokyo: Japan Society for the Promotion of Science.

Hashimoto, Anne Yue. 1971. *Mandarin syntactic structures*. Princeton University.

Haspelmath, Martin. 2002. *Understanding morphology*. London: Arnold.

Hasselgård, Hilde; Johansson, Stig & Lysvåg, Per. 1999. *English grammar. Theory and use*. Oslo: Universitetsforlaget.

Hibiya, Junko. n.d. Diachronic change in sequential voicing. [http://www.let.leidenuniv.nl/ulcl/faculty/vdweijer/jvoice/hibiya.pdf]

Hoekstra, Eric. 1991. *Licensing conditions on phrase structure*. Ph.D., University of Groningen.

Hong, Chai-Song & Lee, Seong-heon. 2003. Representation of lexico-syntactic information for the description of predicate nouns in the Sejong Electronic Dictionary. In: Lee, Sang-Oak, ed. *Korean &/or corpus linguistics*. Seoul: International Circle of Korean Linguistics. 249-274.

Hou, John. 1979. Grammatical relations in Chinese. Ph.D., University of Southern California.

Hsu, Kylie. 2002. *Selected issues in Mandarin Chinese word structure analysis*. Lewiston: Edwin Mellen Press.

Hualde, José Ignacio. 1992. *Catalan*. London: Routledge.

Hualde, José Ignacio & Ortiz de Urbina, Jon. 2003. *A grammar of Basque*. Berlin/New York: Mouton de Gruyter.

Irwin, Mark. 2009. Prosodic size and rendaku immunity. *Journal of East Asian Linguistics* 18. 179-196.

Iwasaki, Shoichi. 2002. Prioperceptive-state expressions in Thai. *Studies in Language* 26:1. 33-66.

Iwasaki, Shoichi & Ingkaphirom, Preeya. 2005. *A reference grammar of Thai*. Cambridge: Cambridge University Press.

Jacob, Daniel. 2003. Pour une nouvelle définition des fonctions des cas. *Syntaxe et Sémantique* 4. 47-66.

Jaisser, Annie. 1990. DeLIVERing an introduction to psycho-collocations with SIAB in White Hmong. *Linguistics of the Tibeto-Burman Area* 13:1. 159-178.

Jun, Sun-Ah. 1995. Asymmetrical effects on the laryngeal gesture in Korean. In: Connel, Bruce & Arvaniti, Amalia, eds. *Phonology and phonetic evidence: Papers in laboratory phonology IV*. Cambridge: Cambridge University Press. 235-253.

Kageyama, Tarō. 1993. *Bunpō to gokeisei* [Grammar and word-formation]. Hitsuji Shoin.

Kageyama, Tarō. 1999. Word formation. In: Tsujimura, Naoko, ed. *The handbook of Japanese linguistics*. Malden: Blackwell. 297-325.

Kang, Eungyeong. 2002. Edge-Integrity and the syllable structure in Korean. In: *Proceedings of the 16th Pacific-Asia Conference on Language, Information, and Computation*. The Society of Korean Information Society. Seoul, Korea. 135-146.

Kang, Shin. 2004. *Hyentaymongkole yenkwu* [Research on Modern Mongolian]. Seoul: Mwunyeylim.

Kang, Sun-Young. 1997. Unaccusative verbs in Korean: with a special reference to the verbs *ci-* and *toy-*. *Sayngseng munpep yenkwu* 7:2. 115-152.

Keenan, Edward L. 1976. Toward a universal definition of 'subject'. In: Li, Charles, ed. *Subject and topic*. New York: Academic Press. 303-333.

Kim, Jung-eun. 1995. *Kwuke tane hyengsengpep yenkwu* [Research on word-formation in Korean]. Seoul: Pagijong.

Kim, Chin-Woo. 1970. Boundary phenomena in Korean. *Papers in Linguistics* 2. 1-26.

Kim, Jung-Ho. 2003. Hitaikaku dōshi no dekigoto kōzō: kannichi ryōgengo no hikaku taishō no kanten kara [The event structure of unaccusative verbs: A comparative study of Korean and Japanese]. *Gengo kagaku ronshū* 7. 35-45.

Kim, Moo-Rim. 2002. Kwuke umwun hyensangui sengkyekkwa pemwi: umwunpwuwa ehwuipwuui kwucoey kwanlyenhaye [A classification of the phonological phenomena in Korean]. In: *Korean linguistics today and tomorrow*. Seoul: Hankook. 730-740.

Kim, Jeong-Eun. 1995. *Kwuke tane hyengsengpep yenkwu* [A study on Modern Korean word formation]. Seoul: Pagijong.

Kim, Young-Seok. 1985. *Aspects of Korean morphology*. Seoul: Pan Korea Book Corporation.

Kim, Young-Joo. 1990. *The syntax and semantics of Korean case: the interaction between lexical and syntactic levels of representation*. Ph.D. diss., Harvard University.

Kishimoto, Hideki. 1996. Split intransitivity in Japanese and the unaccusative hypothesis. *Language* 72. 248-286.

Kleiber, Georges. 1991. *Paul est bronzé* versus *La peau de Paul est bronzée*. Contre une approche référentielle analytique. In: Stammerjohann, Harro, ed. *Analyse et synthèse dans les langues romanes et slaves*. Tübingen: Narr. 109-134.

Klingebiel, Kathryn. 1989. *Noun + verb compounding in Western romance*. Berkeley: University of California Press.

Ko, Seongyeon. 2002. *Kwukeuy piumhwawa yuumhwa hyensangey tayhan yenkwu: Choyceksengilonul cwungsimulo* [A study on nasalization and lateralization in Korean: An optimality-theoretic account]. M.A. thesis, Seoul National University.

Komolwanig, Kamol-orn & Naoko Sawada. 1993. A contrastive study of copulative sentences in Japanese and Thai. *Gengo kenkyu* 103. 92-116.

Kratochvíl, Paul. 1968. *The Chinese language today: Features of an emerging standard*. London: Hutchinson University Library.

Kubozono, Haruo. 1995. *Gokeisei to onin kōzō* [Word formation and phonological structures]. Tokyo: Kuroshio.

Kubozono, Haruo. 2005. Rendaku: Its domain and linguistic conditions. In: Weijer, Jeroen van de; Nanjo, Kensuke & Nishihara, Tetsuo, eds. *Voicing in Japanese*. Berlin: Mouton de Gruyter. 5-24.

Kullman, Rita & Tserenpil, D. 1996. *Mongolian grammar*. Ulaanbaatar: Academy of Sciences.

Kuno, Susumu & Johnson, Yuki. 2005. On the non-canonical double nominative construction in Japanese: The particle *ga* as an object marker. *Studies in Language* 29:2. 285-328.

Kuno, Susumu. 1973. *The structure of the Japanese language*. Cambridge: MIT Press.

Kuno, Susumu. 2004. *Studies in Korean syntax and semantics*. Seoul: Pagijong.

Kuno, Susumu & Wongkhomthong, Preya. 1981. Characterizational and identificational sentences in Thai. *Studies in Language* 5:1. 65-109.

Lakoff, George & Johnson, Mark. 2003. *Metaphors we live by*. London: The University of Chicago Press.

Langacker, Ronald W. 1984. Active zones. In: Brugman, C. & Macaulay, M., eds. *Proceedings of the tenth annual meeting of the Berkeley Linguistic Society*. Berkeley: Berkeley Linguistic Society. 172-188.

Langacker, Ronald W. 1987. *Foundations of cognitive grammar*. Stanford: Stanford University Press.

Launay, Michel. 1998. Compound nouns vs. incorporation in classical Nahuatl. *Sprachtypologie und Universalienforschung* 52:3/4. 347-364.

Lazard, Gilbert. 1998. *Actancy*. Berlin: Mouton de Gruyter.

Lee, Hyun-Bok. 1989. *Korean grammar*. Oxford: Oxford University Press.

Lee, Ik-Sop & Ramsey, S. Robert. 2000. *The Korean language*. New York: State University of New York Press.

Lee, Junkyu & Lee, Chungmin. 2003. Korean resultative constructions. In: *Proceedings of the 9th International Conference on Head-Driven Phrase Structure Grammar*. Stanford: CSLI. 169-186.

Lee, Keedong. 1993. *A Korean grammar on semantic-pragmatic principles*. Seoul: Hankwukmunhwasa.

Lee, Sun-Hee; Jang, Seok Bae & Seo, Sang Kyu. 2017. *A frequency dictionary of Korean*. London: Routledge.

Lehonkoski, Ritva. 2000. *Describing East Asian grammar*. Helsinki.

Lemaréchal, Alain. 2001. Mais à quoi peut donc bien servir la copule? In: Buridant, Claude; Kleiber, Georges & Pellat, Jean-Christophe, éd. *Par monts et par vaux: Itinéraires linguistiques et grammaticaux. Mélanges Martin Riegel*. Paris/Louvain: Peeters. 235-242.

Lemaréchal, Alain. 1998. *Études de morphologie en f(x, ...)*. Louvain: Peeters.

Levin, Beth & Rappaport Hovav, Malka. 1995. *Unaccusativity: At the syntax-lexical semantics interface*. Cambridge: MIT Press.

Lewandowski, Theodor. 1990. *Linguistisches Wörterbuch* (Bd. I). Heidelberg: Quelle Meyer.

Li, Charles N. & Thompson, Sandra A. 1981. *Mandarin Chinese: A functional reference grammar*. Berkeley: University of California Press.

Lieber, Rochelle. 1992. *Deconstructing morphology*. Chicago: University of Chicago Press.

Lloyd, Paul M. 1968. *Verb-complement compounds in Spanish*. Tübingen: Max Niemeyer.

Lüdtke, Jens. 2005. *Romanische Wortbildung: Inhaltlich, diachronisch, synchronisch*. Tübingen: Stauffenburg Verlag.

Lyman, Benjamin S. 1894. Change from surd to sonant in Japanese compounds. *Oriental Studies of the Oriental Club of Philadelphia*. 1-17.

Marantz, Alec. 1984. *On the nature of grammatical relations*. Cambridge: MIT Press.

Martin, Samuel E. 1954. *Korean morphophonemics*. Baltimore: Linguistic Society of America.

Martin, Samuel E. 1992. *A reference grammar of Korean*. Rutland: Tuttle.

Matisoff, James. 1986. Hearts and minds in South-east Asian languages and English: An essay in the comparative lexical semantics of psycho-collocations. *Cahiers de linguistique Asie Orientale* 15:1. 5-57.

Mikami, Akira. 1960. *Zô wa hana ga nagai*. Tokyo: Kuroshio.

Mithun, Marianne. 1984. The evolution of noun incorporation. *Language* 60. 847-894.

Mithun, Marianne. 2000. Incorporation. In: Booij, Geert & al., eds. *Morphologie/Morphology*. Berlin: Walter de Gruyter. 916-928.

Miyagawa, Shigeru. 1989. Light verbs and the ergative hypothesis. *Linguistic Inquiry* 20. 659-668.

Mok, Jung-Soo. 2005. Kwuke icwungcwue kwumunuy saylowun haysek [A new Interpretation of the double-subject construction in Korean]. *Enehak* 41. 75-99.

Motoori, Norinaga. [1790-1822. *Kojiki-den* [Commentaries on the Kojiki]. Edo: Maegawa rokuzaemon.

Na, Younghee. 1986. The conventionalization of semantic distinctions. In: *Papers from the 22nd Regional Meeting Chicago Linguistic Society*. 166-178.

Nam, Jee-Sun. 1996. *Classification syntaxique des constructions adjectivales en coréen*. Amsterdam: John Benjamins.

Nam, Ki-Shim. 2005. *Modern Korean syntax*. Seoul: Thaehaksa.

Nedjalkov, Igor. 1997. *Evenki*. London: Routledge.

Nedjalkov, Vladimir P. 1976. Diathesen und Satzstruktur im Tschuktschischen. In: Lötsch, R. & Růžička, R., eds. *Satzstruktur und Genus Verbi*. Berlin: Akademie Verlag. 181-211.

Nomura, Masaaki. 1977. Zōgohō [Word formation]. In: *Iwanami kōza, nihongo 9: goi to imi*. Tokyo: Iwanami shoten. 245-284.

Osumi, Midori. 1995. *Tinrin grammar*. Honolulu: University of Hawai'i Press.

Packard, Jerome Lee. 1998. A lexical phonology of Mandarin Chinese. In: Packard, J. L., ed. *New approaches to Chinese word formation*. Mouton de Gruyter. 311-327.

Packard, Jerome Lee. 2000. *The morphology of Chinese: A linguistic and cognitive approach.* Cambridge: Cambridge University Press.

Paillard, Michel. 2007. Du pickpocket au vide-poche. Remarques sur les composés verbe-objet en français et en anglais. *Travaux linguistiques du Cerlico* 20. 159-171.

Park, Byung-Soo. 2001. Constraints on multiple nominative constructions in Korean: A constraint-based lexicalist approach. *Enekwahak yenkwu* 20. 147-190.

Park, Chulwoo. 2002. Kwukeui pochwungewa pwukae phanpyel kicwun [Criteria for distinguishing complements and adjuncts in Korean]. *Enehak* 34. 75-111.

Paul, Waltraud. 1988. *The syntax of verb-object phrases in Chinese: constraints and reanalysis.* Paris: Editions Regards Croisés.

Perlmutter, David. 1978. Impersonal passives and the Unaccusative Hypothesis. In: *Proceedings of the Fourth Annual Meeting of the Berkeley Linguistic Society.* Berkeley: University of California. 257-289.

Polinsky, Maria S. 1990. Subject incorporation: evidence from Chukchee. In: Dziwirek, Katarzyna; Farrell, Patrick & Mejías-Bikandi, Errapel, eds. *Grammatical relations: A cross-theoretical perspective.* Stanford: CSLI. 349-364.

Polinsky, Maria S. 1993. Subject inversion and intransitive subject incorporation. In: *Proceedings of CLS 29.* Chicago Linguistics Society. 343-361.

Post, Mark. 2007. Grammaticalisation and compounding in Thai and Chinese: a text-frequency approach. *Studies in Language* 31:1. 117-175.

Post, Mark. 2008. Adjectives in Thai: Implications for a functionalist typology of word classes. *Linguistic Typology* 12:3. 339-381.

Pottelberge, Jeroen van. 2007. Funktionsverbgefüge und verwandte Erscheinungen. In: Burger, Harald & al., eds. *Phraseologie/Phraseology. An international handbook of contemporary research,* Vol. 2. Berlin: Walter de Gruyter. 436-444.

Rijk, Rudolph P. G. 2008. *Standard Basque: A progressive grammar.* Cambridge: The MIT Press.

Rodriguez, João. 1603. *Vocabvlario da lingoa de Iapam.* Nangasaqui: Companhia de Iesu.

Roussarie, Laurence & Villoing, Florence. 2003. Some semantic investigations on the French VN construction. In: *GL 2003, 2nd international workshop on generative approaches to the lexicon, Genève.* 130-137.

Sadock, Jerrold. 2006. Noun incorporation. In: Brown, Keith, ed. *Encyclopedia of language and linguistics,* 2nd edn. Oxford: Elsevier. 584-587.

Sangati, Federico & Mazza, Chiara. 2009. An English dependency treebank à la Tesnière. In: Proceedings TLT8, December 09. n.p.

Scalise, Sergio. 1992. Compounding in Italian. *Rivista di Linguistica* 4:1. 175-199.

Scalise, Sergio. 1994. *Morfologia*. Bologna: Il Mulino.

Schapira, Charlotte. 1985. Les composés roumains à thème verbal, et leur place dans l'ensemble des langues romanes. *Revue de linguistique romane* 49. 15-26.

Shibatani, Masayoshi. 1990. *The languages of Japan*. Cambridge: Cambridge University Press.

Shibatani, Masayoshi. 2001. Non-canonical constructions in Japanese. In: Aikhenvald, Alexandra Y.; Dixon, Robert Malcom Ward & Onishi, Masayuki, eds. *Non-canonical marking of subjects and objects*. Amsterdam: John Benjamins. 307-354.

Sneddon, James Neil. 2000. *Understanding Indonesian grammar: A student's reference and workbook*. St. Leonards: Allen Unwin.

Sohn, Ho-Min. 1986. *Linguistic expeditions*. Seoul: Hanshin.

Sohn, Ho-Min. 1999. *The Korean language*. Cambridge: Cambridge University Press.

Song, Jae Jung. 2005. *The Korean language: Structure, use, and context*. London: Routledge.

Spencer, Andrew. 1999. Chukchee homepage. [url: http://privatewww.essex.ac.uk/ ~spena/Chukchee/CHUKCHEE_HOMEPAGE.html]

Spencer, Andrew. 2005. Word-formation and syntax. In: Štekauer, Pavol & Lieber, Rochelle, eds. *Handbook of word-formation*. Dordrecht: Springer. 73-97.

Su, Yi-Ching. 1999. The representation of compounds and phrases in the mental lexicon: Evidence from Chinese. *Web Journal of Modern Language Linguistics* 1. [http://wjmll.ncl.ac.uk/issue04-05/su.htm]

Sugetta, Shigeaki. 1992. I nomi composti <verbo+nome> in italiano moderno. In: Moretti, Bruno; Petrini, Dario; Bianconi, Sandro, eds. *Linee di tendenza dell'italiano contemporaneo. Atti del XXV Congresso della Società di Linguistica Italiana*. Roma: Bulzoni. 217-222.

Sugioka, Yoko. 1984. *Interaction of derivational morphology and syntax in Japanese and English*. Ph.D., University of Chicago.

Suzuki, Yutaka. 2008. Dōshi renyōkei tensei meishi o kōbuyōso to suru fukugōgo no rendaku [Rendaku in compounds whose second element is a deverbal noun]. *Bunkyo gakuin daigaku Kiyō* 8. 213-234.

Takada, Hareo. 2008. *Le mot composé: étude contrastive de certains types de mots composés japonais et français*. Niigata: Université de Niggata.

Takahashi, Kiyoko & Shinzato, Rumiko. 2003. On Thai copulas, khUU1 and pen1: A cognitive approach. In: *Proccedings of the 2nd Seoul International Conference on Discourse and Cognitive Linguistics: Discourse and Cognitive Perspectives on Human Language*. 131-145.

Tamura, Suzuko. 1999. *The Ainu language*. Tokyo: Sanseido.

Tang, Ting-chi. 1972. *A case grammar of spoken Chinese*. Taipei: Hai-guo.

Teng, Shou-Hsin. 1974. Double nominative in Chinese. *Language* 50:3. 455-472.

Tesnière, Lucien. 1959. *Éléments de syntaxe structurale*. Paris: Klincksieck.

Tollemache, Federico. 1945. *Le parole composte nella lingua italiana*. Roma.

Tomić Mišeska, Olga. 1998. *The English word*. Novi Sad: Futura Publikacije.

Toratani, Kiyoko. 1997. *Typology of split-intransitivity: lexical aspect and the unaccusative hypothesis in Japanese*. M.A., University of Buffalo.

Tsunoda, Tasaku. 1995. The possession cline in Japanese and other languages. In: Chappell, H. & McGregor, W., eds. *The Grammer of Inalienability*. Berlin: Moutoan de Gruyter. 565-630.

Tuggy, David H. 1987. Scarecrow nouns, generalizations, and cognitive grammar. In: DeLancey, Scott & Tomlin, Russell S., eds. *Proceedings of the Third Annual Meeting of the Pacific Linguistics Conference*. 307-320.

Tuggy, David H. 2003. 'Abrelatas' and 'Scarecrow' nouns: Exocentric verb-noun compounds as illustrations of basic principles of cognitive grammar. *International Journal of English Studies* 3:2. 25-61.

Vance, Timothy. 1987. *An introduction to Japanese phonology*. Albany: State University of New York Press.

Verdaguer, Pere. 1999. *Grammaire de la langue catalane*. Barcelona: Curial.

Villoing, Florence. 2002. *Les mots composés [VN]N/A du français: réflexions épistémologiques et propositions d'analyse*. Ph.D., Université Paris X-Nanterre.

Villoing, Florence. 2003. Les mots composés VN du français: arguments en faveur d'une construction morphologique. *Cahiers de grammaire* 28. 183-196.

Webelhuth, Gert. 1995. Idioms, patterns and anthropocentricity. In: Aranovich, Paul & al., eds. *Proceedings of the Thirteen West Coast Conference on Formal Linguistics*. Center for the Study of Language and Information: Stanford Linguistics Association. 400-415.

Widłak, Stanisław. 1991. De l'analytique au synthétique: Les mots composés en italien. Quelques remarques. In: Stammerjohann, Harro, ed. *Analyse et synthèse dans les langues romanes et slaves*. Tübingen: Narr. 185-192.

Wierzbicka, Anna. 1976. Mind and body. In: McCawley, J. D., ed. *Syntax and semantic 7: Notes from the linguistic underground*. New York: Academic Press. 129-157.

Yeon, Jaehoon. 1986. *Hankwuke tonsaseng myengsa hapsenge.uy coepep kwa uymi yenkwu* [The formation and meaning of verbal compounds in Korean]. Seoul National University.

Yeon, Jaehoon. 1989. Hankwuke cwunglip tongsa kwumuney tayhan yenkwu [A study on the neutral-verb construction in Korean]. *Hangeul* 203. 165-188.

Yeon, Jaehoon. 1993. The degree of transitivity in Korean: A functional-typological approach. *Language Research* 29:1. 107-136.

Yip, Po-Ching. 2000. *The Chinese lexicon: A comprehensive survey.* New York: Routledge.

Zhang, Jin. 2011. L2 Acquisition of Chinese locative inversion. In: *Proceedings of the 23rd North American Conference on Chinese Lingusitics (NACCL-23), 2011.* 250-261.

Index